The Haunted South

Other University of South Carolina Press Books

by Nancy Roberts

South Carolina Ghosts:
From the Coast to the Mountains

Ghosts of the Carolinas

Ghosts of the Southern
Mountains and Appalachia

The Gold Seekers:
*Gold, Ghosts, and Legends from
Carolina to California*

North Carolina Ghosts
& Legends

Civil War Ghost
Stories & Legends

The Haunted South

Where Ghosts Still Roam

By Nancy Roberts

University of South Carolina Press

Published in Columbia, South Carolina, by the
University of South Carolina Press

Originally published in 1970 as *This Haunted Southland*
Also published as *This Haunted Southland: Where Ghosts Still Roam*

Manufactured in the United States of America

02 01 00 99   8 7 6 5

The Library of Congress has cataloged the cloth edition as follows:

Roberts, Nancy, 1924–

       p.   cm.
       Reprint. Originally published: This haunted land. lt ed.
Charlotte, N.C.: McNally and Loftin, 1970
       ISBN 0-87249-588-4 (hard back)
       1. Tales—Southern States. 2. Ghosts—Southern States
I. Title.
GR108.R63   1988
398.2'5'0975—dc19   88-26096

Photographs by Bruce Roberts

ISBN 0-87249-589-2 (pbk.)

Contents

Prologue

We believe there are spirits who walk this land and we would like to introduce some of them to you as you read this book.

They are the spirits of the people, both good and bad, who forded the rivers, climbed the hills and cultivated the fields which are our inheritance—men and women who loved and fought and gave the land we call "home" names like Gold Hill, Kings Mountain and Wizard Clip.

Housing developments now cover the countryside where hundreds of miners, many from foreign lands, once worked in the Carolina gold fields. Modern highways slash through hills where King George's men stood in resplendent battle lines. But the builders and developers have only destroyed the physical appearance of the area. They can never kill the ghosts and spirits which must rise at night as surely as does the full moon.

And the supernatural is far from remote. It is a matter of daily experience for those who look for more than mediums and witchcraft can never offer.

C. S. Lewis once said, "There is no neutral ground in the universe. Every square inch, every split second, is claimed by God and counterclaimed by Satan." The spirits in this book have fought for both sides and there are others who don't appear to have been on any particular side, but dazed by death and perchance in some sort of limbo, they still return to the land they knew in life.

The ghosts in these pages have an attachment for certain places and when you read these stories, we hope you will understand why. For they do not respect the deed books at the county court house. This is THEIR land and they plan to be here through countless centuries, if they so choose. For a time we feared that progress would eliminate spirits but now that we know them better, we become more convinced that the spirits will not only endure, but will outlast "progress."

Bruce and Nancy Roberts
February 4, 1971

P.S. For those who don't believe in ghosts we have a remedy. The first night of the full moon in October walk to the top of Kings Mountain and then down the path to Colonel Ferguson's grave. Spend the next night watching the Brown Mountain lights alone from a deserted overlook on the Blue Ridge Parkway. And, on the third night go alone at midnight to the Devil's Tramping Ground near Siler City and wait for the moon to set. This will help restore your faith.

The Haunted South

Passenger Train Number 9

She was sure she had seen a horrible train wreck, but the stationmaster said there had not been a wreck

Do people have premonitions of fearful events which are going to happen to them in the future? How can we tell how often premonitions like this come true, especially if the people are no longer here to tell us.

The baggage master was a tall thin man with a prominent nose and fair skin so transparent the bony structure of his face could be plainly seen beneath it. His eyebrows were a sandy color tipped with gray and the blue eyes which peered out from beneath them had a surprising degree of sparkle and humor. Right now he was scrutinizing his watch observing that it was almost one o'clock in the morning and satisfied that all the baggage was loaded and the train would be leaving Salisbury for Asheville, North Carolina, in a few minutes.

The steam engine spewed forth smoke and cinders, the cry of the whistle was a thin, earsplitting shriek in the stillness of the early morning. The baggage master's name was H. K. Linster and he was from Statesville where he usually got off for a few minutes to chat with friends. He frowned as he snapped the case of his large lavishly engraved gold watch shut and prepared to board the train. Was there a hint of reluctance in his step? Did he feel any differently tonight than on the hundreds of nights before?

But that was many years ago, early morning of August 27th, 1891 to be exact, and our story has more to do with the summer vacation trip of a family from Columbia, S.C.

There was nothing unusual about the way it all started. Pat and Larry Hayes had been planning their mountain vacation for a long time. Not that they could really afford a trip what with Larry having only been in business for himself a year, but they both knew the whole family needed it.

The borrowed camper would save money and although Pat knew little about camping, she was game to learn and the children were old enough to help. Larry was not through work until late and it was after ten when Pat put the extra bedding in the trunk and they were ready to go. Larry decided he would let Pat drive from Columbia, South Carolina, to Charlotte, North Carolina, and he would drive the next lap to Statesville which was not far from Pat's mother's home.

At the filling station where they stopped in Charlotte, the station attendant commented that one of the tires was low and Larry agreed that he should fill it with more air. By now the children were asleep and Pat laid her silver blonde head back on a pillow wedged between the seat and the door so that she could nap.

Larry drove silently, following the road almost automatically, while his thoughts were on the past year and his efforts to build up his business. Sud-

denly, he felt the wheel twist beneath his hand and the car begin to go toward the other side of the road. He realized the tire had blown and the weight of the trailer was making it more difficult for him to control the car. Pat was immediately awake but she did not scream or cry out. Luckily he managed to slow the car, guide it back into his own lane and off the road onto the safety of the shoulder.

Larry got out to look for the jack so that he could change the tire. He and Pat both searched the back of the car but no jack. Then Pat remembered. She had left the jack on the floor of the garage when she rearranged the camping supplies.

It was almost three o'clock in the morning, there were no cars along the road at this hour and Larry figured the best thing to do was to go for help. He remembered a country store he had noticed just before the blowout. There was a light on in the back and he suspected the store owner might live there.

The children complained drowsily, then one by one fell asleep again. Pat sat wide awake and somewhat nervous but reassured by Larry's certainty that it was only a short distance back to the store.

She heard the whistle of a train far off in the distance and as it came closer she thought of how mournful a train whistle late at night can sound. Then a light appeared, at first no bigger than a pinpoint, and she watched it advance closer and closer until it was just a few hundred yards from the car.

It was the headlight on the engine and she could now see the engine and the coaches quite clearly. The train had begun to cross the bridge and had just reached the center when she was aghast to see the engine, cab and coaches give a convulsive lurch, leave the track and hurtle through the air, plunging off the bridge down into the darkness and out of sight. There were crashing, wrenching sounds as metal and wood tore asunder and cars smashed against each other.

This was followed by the most frightful screams, men's and women's voices intermingled, pleading for help. Horror-stricken, Pat jumped out of the car and began running in the direction from which the screams came. When she reached the bank of the stream and looked down below her, it was a sickening sight. The engine, tender, coaches and pullman cars were a huge pile of debris jutting out in every direction and completely damming up the creek.

People were climbing through broken windows, some being pulled through by those who had crawled out first and there were yet others who had fallen into the stream and were trying to swim to the bank. Adding to the danger and perilous situation of survivors was the fact that, dammed up by the wreckage, the water in the stream was rising and entering the railroad cars.

In the midst of all the cries and groans Pat became aware that there was a man standing next to her. He was dressed in what must have been a railroad uniform and beneath the visor of his hat she could see that his face looked extremely white. No wonder, after what this poor man had just gone through.

"Can you give me the time, Ma'am? I would like to check my watch and see if it is running properly," said the trainman. He was gazing down at a large gold watch which she noticed with surprise looked just like the old-fashioned watch her grandfather used to show her when she was a child. But no doubt, railroad men still carried watches like this.

"It is five minutes past three," she replied. "I wish I could go for help, but we just had a blowout and I will have to wait until my husband comes back." The man looked at her strangely and did not answer. She began to feel very much afraid. Then his face started to blur and she thought, I must be going to faint, that is why his face seems to be fading away like this.

At that moment she heard the slam of a car door and voices behind her. There was Larry and someone was with him. She ran toward them.

"Larry, there's been a terrible train wreck!" she cried out. Larry and the stranger held a flashlight before them and the three made their way as quickly as possible in the direction she led them over at the side of the bridge. They looked down.

16

"Where? What in the world are you talking about? There's no train wreck down there," said Larry, the beam of his flashlight probing the stream and the banks.

"For heaven's sake, honey, you've just had some kind of nightmare. This is Mr. Bradley. He's come to help me fix the tire. Come on now, let's go back to the car. You probably fell asleep and when you woke up your dream was real to you."

Dazed, Pat got into the car, and checked the children. They were still asleep, completely unaware that anything unusual had happened.

On the way to her mother's home, Pat told Larry about seeing the train approach, the horrifying wreck and the trainman who had come up to the car. He promised to go by the railroad station the next morning and, if she wished, even back to where she was so certain she had seen the wreck. Larry was still convinced, however, that she had fallen asleep and dreamed about the wreck and the trainman who had asked her what time it was.

The next day they went by the railroad station. The old man at the counter listened while Pat told him about the train going off the track.

"No, there was no wreck last night. There hasn't been a wreck in years on that stretch of track."

"At least not since the wreck of 1891," he said. "My father used to talk about that wreck. It was the most terrible train wreck that ever happened in this state. The train had left Salisbury for Asheville and it got to Bostian's Bridge about three o'clock in the morning. It must have been a dreadful sight to see. They say the train engine and coaches just plunged right off the track and down ninety feet into the stream below the trestle. My father got out there pretty soon and he saw people climbing out the windows and calling for help. But what made it even worse was the coaches dammed up the stream and lots of those people drowned."

"It happened . . . let's see. That's odd. Looks like it was about fifty year ago. I think there's a clipping from an old paper called The Charlotte *Chronicle* in a scrapbook in my drawer."

He rummaged in the drawer, producing a scrapbook full of clippings about promotions, retirement pictures, buildings renovations and other miscellaneous news affecting the railroad over a period of many years. Finally, he came to a yellowed clipping from The Charlotte *Chronicle* of August 28, 1891. It was headlined, "Hurled to Death, Thirty Killed, Many Injured. At Three O'clock in the Morning, Bridge Near Statesville The Scene of the Wreck."

"You know the baggage master, a man named H. K. Linster from right here in Statesville, was killed in the wreck. He usually got off and chatted with my dad for a few minutes. What a terrible thing that must have been. I sure would hate to have seen it."

Pat Hayes' face turned white and her head began to swim. It seemed that the inside of the railroad station was beginning to go around and around. She held on to the edge of the counter and closed her eyes for a minute. But that was worse! For then she could see the light of a train followed by the engine and the coaches as they twisted and lurched before they hurtled off the track and down into the darkness. The lights in the coaches streaked through her mind like fireworks going off and again and again she could hear the screams.

18

"Lady, lady, are you all right?" The station master was holding her elbow.

"I didn't mean to upset you none. After all, that wreck happened fifty years ago. In fact, it was exactly fifty years ago last night."

The Little People

"I saw them with my own eyes. They were on the mountain, they were near the rock . . . they were everywhere!"

There are still some wild and unexplored places left in the mountains of Western North Carolina and one about which many weird tales continue to be told is Hickory Nut Gorge near Chimney Rock.

The gorge is a challenge to even the most bold and experienced. There are precipitate cliffs, narrow ledges to scale and dizzying heights, and the reward may be bottomless pools, spectacular waterfalls seen by few and grotesque rock formations.

Nor far from this gorge on the thirty-first of July 1806, a Presbyterian minister and teacher at Newton Academy sat at his desk preparing his lesson for the following day's classes. He was so absorbed in his work that it was almost eight o'clock when he realized the light had gone and the pleasant breeze which had stirred the curtains at the window next to his desk now had an icy bite.

He closed the window, found the white china matchbox, lit the kerosene lamps and touched a match to the fire. As the flames blazed up he heard

Chimney Rock where the Little People were seen on several occasions

footsteps on the porch and an agitated pounding at his door.

Hurrying through the dark hall he bumped into the sharp, curving arms of the coat rack on his way to the front door. When he opened it there stood his friend, Robert Searcy.

"I don't know how to tell you what I have just seen" said Searcy. "You may not even believe me, but I saw them with my own eyes. They were on the mountain, they were near the rock, they were everywhere! May I come in and sit down?" His face was white and he appeared genuinely shaken.

"Of course, you may. But who in the world are you talking about and what have you seen?"

"Well, no matter how I tell you about this it is going to sound like I have lost my mind, but probably the best thing for me to do is start at the beginning. As I sat on my porch reading after an early supper, Mrs. Reaves' girl came running up to tell me there was a crowd of people flying around on the side of the mountain near the Rock and to come right away. I simply dismissed what she said as probably some children playing a prank.

"But a few minutes later Mrs. Reaves herself came and begged me to go with her to see the 'ghosties' as she called them. This poor superstitious woman is really upset, I told myself, and deciding that the kindest thing I could do was to go with her to calm her, we started toward the mountain. After a few minutes she said, 'Do you see them?'

"I saw nothing at all and told her so. We walked a little further and she grasped my arm saying, 'There they are. Look! Over there.' This time as I looked toward the Chimney, I was absolutely amazed for south of Chimney Rock and floating along the side of the mountain was a huge crowd of white, phantom-like beings. Their clothing, and filmy as it looked, I can only call it 'clothing,' was so brilliant a white it almost hurt my eyes to look at them. But they appeared to be human, for I could see that there were men and women and children, all sizes of beings, even infants.

"As I watched, two of them who appeared to be men went on ahead of the crowd, coming quite close to the Rock, and then vanished."

"What a frightening experience," said Newton.

"No, that is the oddest part of it," replied Searcy. "Although I felt weak, somehow, it left a solemn and

pleasing impression on my mind. But you must think I have surely gone crazy. Tell me, is that what has happened? Is this the beginning of some strange insanity?"

Robert Searcy searched his friend's face anxiously for an answer. Smoke curled upward from Newton's pipe. He frowned thoughtfully and looked toward the window with its drawn curtains as if he were trying to see through them and out to the gorge for a glimpse of the mysterious beings Searcy had described.

"Don't just sit there! Tell me, friend. Am I going insane?" shouted Searcy.

"No, no. Now calm down," Newton raised one hand palm outward toward his friend. "You are not going crazy at all. You have simply seen a sight that only a few people have ever been privileged to witness. A sight so spectacular that stories about it have been told for generations among the Cherokee Indians. You recall that this whole area was once the country of the Cherokee Nation."

"For heavens sake, George, do I need a history lesson at a time like this? What does that have to do with the white figures I saw floating along the mountainside?"

"I am telling you this because the Cherokees knew about them."

"Knew about who?"

"The Little People. Do you think that something like you saw this afternoon has never happened before? Of course it has. Rare, yes, and it may have been years ago and it may not happen for many years hence."

"The gorge was the gateway to the country where the tobacco the Indians wanted for their pipes grew. It was always a frightening place to the Indians, but it was not so much the difficulties of travelling through it, the bottomless pools, the eerie rock formations which appear to us like frightful giants of another age. Nor was it the savage force with which the wind sweeps through that gorge, tearing away plants and leaving the rock bare. Oh, no. It was not these things that kept them from travelling through the gorge to reach the land where the tobacco grew. It was the spirits, the little people themselves or whatever you wish to call them, that guarded the gateway through the mountains."

"Tonight you have seen what no man may see again for years. I don't know how to explain them. You say that you saw men, women and children. If they were a mirage it is strange that a mirage would have stayed in the area long enough for Mrs. Reaves to have sent her daughter, then come after you herself. Also, a mirage is more often seen by one person,

perhaps due to their physical or mental state at the moment, rather than by several."

"Could these 'beings' be angels?" asked Searcy.

"Angels? I really don't know. I have never been a great believer in spirits from another world making themselves visible in our own, but if I had been fortunate enough to see that fantastic crowd

25

of white robed figures floating across the mountain-side as you did this afternoon, I might change my mind!

"You must see it, too. It was tremendous! When do you think it might happen again?"

"My dear Robert, how am I possibly to guess when it will happen again. We have no idea what causes them to appear. But, I would say that it is possible for the same condition present this evening to occur at another time and when they do, whoever is near the Rock will see the figures just as you did."

Mr. Newton's prediction has come true on more than one occasion since.

In 1811 a similar phenomenon was seen. So large was the crowd that some compared it to a battle with "swords flashing" but this was probably inaccurately described. Again, shortly after the Civil War the entire countryside talked of seeing The Little People.

But the phenomenon is reported only rarely and probably when someone does see it, they are reluctant to talk of the experience, especially in these days of technology and the computer.

Some scoffers have suggested that all that was ever seen in the gorge were cloud formations, although we wonder whether intelligent observers can mistake clouds for "men, women and children."

The Phantom Rider
of the Confederacy

The General reached for his pistol and aimed it at the oncoming rider when to his astonishment he saw the scores of bullet holes in the cape which floated in the wind

It is really a shame that Ichabod Crane and the Headless Horseman on the Tarrytown Road in New York ever managed to get so much publicity for the headless horseman. For the horseman there was a trickster who carried a pumpkin under his arm and not a head.

For years while people have been reading about this nonsense up at Tarrytown, they have ignored the real Phantom Rider of the Confederacy who rides a palomino stallion. She wears gossamer garments which float behind her and her blond hair streams in the wind. Both hands grasp the reins as she comes out of the past, is visible only briefly, and vanishes into the darkness as if all the legions of another world were in pursuit.

The main highway South through Arden and Fletcher past the old Calvary Episcopal Church has long since been paved. But this has not stopped the pounding of the palomino's hoofbeat which can be heard on the shoulder of the road.

Reverend Charles Stewart McClellan, Jr., writing in the Southern Tourist Magazine in December 1926, was the first writer to compare the Phantom Rider of the South with the Legend of Sleepy Hollow.

"There is a horseman who often rides through the night around old Calvary Church at Fletcher."

He tells the story of a very beautiful girl who lived near the church and was in love with a Confederate soldier whom her family refused to let her marry. Eventually, her suitor was ordered away to join Braxton Bragg's army at Chattanooga and her parents still held steadfast to their decision that she would never marry a Confederate.

During the days of the war the well at Calvary Church where she met her suitor was called "the wishing well" and local legends said that if you wished hard enough before you drank from the well your wish would come true. Even after he had gone she often went to their meeting place. But the day came when she received word that her beloved had been killed.

So, the story goes that our maiden did not wish to live but only to join the one she loved. Her father paid little heed when she told him her wish would come true and so it did, just as if she had willed her own death.

The evening after the funeral service the Jenkinses sat in silence on the porch of their farm home near Fletcher Road. It was early autumn and the leaves of the dogwood trees, already turned a brilliant red, fluttered in the wind. It appeared as if the air, which was especially cold, came from among the pine trees

in the church yard and the graveyard with its freshly covered grave.

The wind blew in such gusts that a faint chiming sound seemed to come from the church bells. And then in the distance came the pound of hoofbeats. On and on they came. Past the church, past the grave-yard, riding with a strange, inexorable quality straight toward the Jenkins home.

Jenkins had never seen such an awesome sight. The hoofs scarcely seemed to touch the ground. But what terrified him was the palomino horse. For it was the horse of Lieutenant C. A. Walpole and on the horse was a young woman wearing a Confederate cavalry cape to protect her against the cold. He recognized now both the horse and rider. The girl was his daughter buried only the day before and the horse had been sent by the spirit of the young lieutenant to bring her.

Her last wish by the old well had come true.

Directly in front of Jenkins, the horse and its rider stopped. But while the horse stood motionless the wind and dust swirled up in a cloud and from it a voice spoke.

"Father, you have doomed me to ride forever. Do you known how bitter cold the wind is?" and leaves swept fiercely about the horse's hooves.

"Next spring General Stoneman and his troops will be here. They will burn your farm thinking you are a Confederate sympathizer because I will lead them here and they will chase this horse to your barn."

And it came about just as the girl had said. For in the spring of 1865 General Stoneman and his men rode into Fletcher just as dusk was falling across the graveyard and the shadows of the tall pines lay upon the tombstones.

The General was in an angry mood. His advance scouting party had been ambushed on the outskirts of Asheville and the major, who had barely escaped with his life, was describing how he and his men had been lured into the trap chasing a Confederate courier on a palomino horse.

"And the strangest thing happened. Just as the horse was about to pull away from us it turned and started to charge back. I ordered my men to stop and every trooper fired at the rider. The horse reared up as if to laugh at us and then from both sides of the road we were ambushed. Twenty-three of my men were killed. I chased after the rider and I fired my pistol six times. I have never missed my mark before and those bullets went right through him."

General Stoneman was obviously upset and irritated.

"Major, you must be extremely overtired and overwrought. I will dispatch Captain Butler to track down the rider."

A short time later the Captain picked up the trail of a single horse and followed it to a farm not far from Calvary Church. The farm belonged to a man named Jenkins who had died that winter. Butler searched the area but could not find the lone rider. However, he believed that the farm was being used as a refuge by the Confederates so he set fire to not only the house but the buildings around it.

From his headquarters camped at Calvary Church, General Stoneman wandered over to the well. It was past midnight, but the general still could not sleep. It was very seldom any of his men were ambushed and he was puzzled by the conduct of his commanding officer who was noted for his excellent marksmanship.

"I wish I could see that rider myself," he mused as he reached down and picked up the dipper at the well. The instant the water touched his lips he saw flames rising from the Jenkins farmhouse and congratulated himself on a problem solved.

As he turned to walk back across the church yard to his headquarters tent, a dark rider galloped across the field. For a moment he thought it was Butler so he did not call out to the sentries. But the rider did not slow, and then, in a split second, he realized the figure mounted upon the horse was not a Union soldier.

He reached for his pistol and aimed it at the horseman's head when to his astonishment he saw

The iron gates at the end of the church drive never barred the Phantom Rider

that the rider was a woman and there were scores of bullet holes in the cape which floated in the wind behind her. He lowered his gun and watched as horse and rider rushed past him and disappeared down the road. So quickly had the horse come and gone that even the startled sentries had not been able to fire.

There were many things the general knew about war and he was not about to lose another man chasing a ghost. Not a single rider did General Stoneman dispatch to give chase. He looked at the red glow of the flames in the sky and as the road turned and rose at the crest of the hill for a brief second the ghostly rider was silhouetted in the crimson of the horizon. Strangely enough this was the only building ever burned in the Fletcher area.

A few weeks later the war came to a close and the stories of the phantom rider were classified with this period when emotions ran high and violence filled the air.

But, according to Reverend McClellan some years later, two young men of Fletcher were riding along the ridge road one night and one, as he was adjusting his stirrup strap, heard the approach of another horse. As he stood next to his own mount he could clearly see the phantom rider who dashed up to him, gazed curiously at him for a moment, and then galloped away into the night. He also tells of a farmer returning to the Fletcher settlement very late one night who was drowsy and fell asleep on his horse. The horse knew the road and kept on but suddenly the farmer was awakened by the clatter of a horse's hooves.

When he awoke and saw the Rider he sank into unconsciousness and the next day when he came to in his barn, he told his friends the story of his midnight encounter with the Phantom Rider.

And so, there will probably always be accounts of hoofbeats in the night and a mysterious figure on horseback amidst the wooded quiet of Calvary Church, and the old graveyard will continue to provide a refuge for the ghosts of those who frequented this area during its violent and colorful past. A past when the Phantom Rider of the Confederacy, with her cape blown by the wind, sped through the night down the old Fletcher Road, her steed's hoofbeats in the distance coming closer and closer, past the church, past the graveyard, riding on and on and on.

The old Church is still there, the graveyard, the road—and when the night is dark and windy, who knows who else?

The Demon of Wizard Clip

All around them people could hear the
clip-clip of the demoniacal shears

The devil ensnares the sons of men in strange and devious ways. And down to this very day the memory of the evil wrought by one of his minions still hangs like a dank fog over an ancient village in West Virginia.

The village bears three names, Smithfield, Middle-

way and oddest of all—Wizard Clip.

Through it ran the principal wagon route from Baltimore to Southwest Virginia, Kentucky and Tennessee. But the wagoneers have long been dead. With them died the fortunes of Wizard Clip and the man who helped it get its name.

Our story starts near the beginning of the nineteenth century with a Pennsylvanian named Livingstone. Leaving his native state he and his family purchased a lakeside farm on the outskirts of the town we have mentioned. In front of his farm and beside the Opequon River ran the wagon road.

A man of mild temperament, the Pennsylvanian was fond of contrasting with a certain modest air his former failures and the success he was enjoying in his new home.

Although Livingstone himself was liked well enough by his neighbors, the same could not be said of his wife. She was a woman of mean and dominating disposition who kept much to herself.

The Livingstones had lived only a few years in their new home when the event which was to cause their undoing befell them. Appropriately enough it happened on a most miserably cold and rainy night. Gusts of wind screeched plaintively outside the Livingstone's windows and tore with icy fingers at the shutters.

They had readied themselves for bed and were about to ensconce themselves under their feather comforters when Mrs. Livingstone heard a faint sound on the porch, quickly followed by a loud knock.

Her husband went to the door, cautiously cracking it open a few inches, only to have the force of the wind wrest it from his hand. In front of him stood the tall figure of a man, cloak swirling madly about him in the gale.

"I pray you will give me a night's lodging, sir," begged Livingstone's visitor. "My wagon has suffered an accident to a wheel and cannot be repaired before morning."

"We are about to retire but will be glad to have you pass the night with us," replied Livingstone although he could see the dour look on the face of his wife.

The stranger came in and without much grace Mrs. Livingstone showed him to his room.

The house had not been settled and quiet for long when in addition to the eerie wail of the wind another sound could be heard. It was a succession of fearsome groans interspersed with the sharp outcries of a man in pain. Stopping only to jerk on his slippers, Livingstone hurried to the door of the stranger's room and asked him if all was well with him.

In a tortured voice his guest replied that he was deathly ill and did not expect to live to see daylight. He begged his host to summon a Catholic priest that he might be given the last rites, admitting the he had neglected his religion in health, but now, in extremis, felt in dire need of its consolation.

Livingstone replied that he knew of no priest nearby and couldn't hope to find one closer than Maryland. He remarked, however, that his neighbors—the McSherrys and the Minghinis—were Catholic and perhaps could tell him of one.

His wife was by now listening to the conversation and at this she became extremely angry.

"If you think you are going to start out on any such wild goose chase in the middle of the night, I shall take good care to thwart you," said she. "And even if you should succeed in finding one, I warn you, no Romish priest shall ever set foot in my house!"

The turnpike in front of the Livingstone house looked much like this road near Wizard Clip

"The best thing you can do is return to your bed. I'll wager this guest of ours will be as well as you or I by morning. And if I have my way he shall be on his way with the sun's first rays."

Livingstone reluctantly gave in to his wife and went back to bed.

All night the pitiful pleas and outcries continued. Next morning their guest did not appear and, much alarmed, Livingstone entered his room.

The stranger was dead.

Of course, a story had to be decided upon to tell the neighbors. The Livingstones simply said that a wayfarer had asked lodging with them the night before and died in his sleep. They made no mention of his dying wish. They recalled with surprise that he had not told them his name and, search his belongings as they would, no clue could be found to his identity.

A simple funeral was held late the following evening and the unknown traveler laid to rest. The family had no sooner returned home and were gathered around the fire discussing the day's events when the logs in the fireplace began to writhe and jump as if in agony.

Soon they were whirling all about the room in a horrible sort of dance. After them danced Livingstone trying to catch them and heave them back into the fireplace. But no sooner would he return them than what seemed to be an almost demoniacal power would toss them out again.

This went on all night long and the terrified family did not get a moment's rest.

The following morning the worn out Livingstone went down to the highway in front of his house. He had just reached the road when he was accosted by an irate wagoneer who had stopped his team there.

"What the devil do you mean barring a public road with a rope?" cried the fellow. "Untie it from those trees, you rascal."

Livingstone rubbed his tired eyes in bewilderment. He was sure the man was drunk for he could see no rope at all. Becoming more furious by the minute the driver drew a knife and made as if to approach Livingstone. But instead he slashed at the air before him.

Now it was the wagoneer's turn to be amazed. For his knife met no resistance at all. Only airy nothingness. While he stood there in bewilderment debating what to do next another team arrived and its driver went through the same performance with the same outcome.

At length Livingstone mildly suggested that they drive on regardless of the spectre rope, and this they did. But all that day each new arrival brought Livingstone a fresh cursing. And so it kept up for several weeks.

By now it was obvious to the Livingstones and their neighbors that the strange events taking place could only be the work of a demon. And soon the Livingstones began to be harassed in yet another way. A sharp clipping noise as from a pair of invisible shears could be heard throughout and around the house. Worse yet all the family clothes and table linens were cut with crescent-shaped slits.

When visitors arrived to console with the Livingstones they would find even the handkerchiefs folded in their pockets covered with the crescent shaped tears. And all around them they could hear the incessant clip-clip of the demoniacal shears.

On one occasion a lady visitor was complimenting Mrs. Livingstone on the fine flock of ducks waddling through the yard on their way to the Opequon River. "Clip-Clip" went the uncanny, invisible shears and, one after another, each duck's head fell to the ground, cleanly decapitated before the ladies' very eyes.

Stories of the "Wizard Clip" were spreading far and wide. And the young men of the neighborhood, eager to show how fearless they were, talked Livingstone into letting them hold a dance there. Despite the terrors of the place curiosity led many young ladies to attend.

One blustering fellow came all the way from Winchester carrying his rifle. He was determined to show off his bravery to his girl and bragged of what he would do to anything trying to clip him. All went smoothly for awhile when suddenly "clip-clip" went the devilish shears and the Winchester hero felt something flap against the back of his legs.

Much to his humiliation he was forced to retreat backwards through the nearest door while the girls looked coyly in another direction.

By this time poor Livingstone was rapidly losing heart and even his wife's masculine courage was dwindling. One night he had a dream.

He thought he was standing at the foot of a hill on top of which stood a man dressed in flowing black robes. The man appeared to be engaged in some sort of religious ceremony. As he looked at him he became aware of the presence of a disembodied voice near him. The voice whispered that the man on the hill could relieve him of the torture he and his family were undergoing.

Believing the garb to be that of a priest, Livingstone immediately sought aid from the Minghinis and the McSherrys. He found that a certain Father Cahill would shortly be at Shepherdstown, about ten miles away, to hold Catholic services.

His neighbors promised Livingstone an introduction to the priest and on the day specified they accompanied their unhappy neighbor to the church meeting.

Livingstone recognized the priest immediately as the figure in his dream and falling down on his knees begged him for help. As tears streamed down his face he poured out the story of his heartlessness toward the stranger and all that had happened thereafter.

Cahill was a big-fisted Irishman not averse to an encounter even with the devil himself. So he consented to accompany Livingstone and do all he could to relieve him.

When he arrived at the Livingstones' home Father Cahill got down on his knees and, holding a small cross in his hands, prayed fervently. Then he sprinkled holy water on the threshold of the house.

"Now you must take me to the place the stranger

is buried," said the priest. Together they went to what is now the old burying ground of Wizard Clip.

As the priest consecrated the grave there was the sound of a great rushing wind through the trees overhead. His robes billowed out from his body, lending an eerie, winged look to the blackgarbed figure.

And the bottomless waters of the nearby lake seethed turbulently as if embracing its own. Close to the village of Wizard Clip the dark waters still hold their secret. The wizard is gone but somehow one has the feeling he may not be far off. And if walking through the village on a rainy afternoon about dusk doesn't convince you the story is true then go to the county clerk's office in Charles Town, West Virginia.

There in the yellowing deed book is the very paper whereby in gratitude to Father Cahill and his successors Livingstone deeded thirty-four acres of land for the exorcising of the fiend. To this day the land is known as "Priest's Field."

43

Room for One More

*The coachman called "room for one more,"
and this time the invitation seemed to
be meant for her!*

It seemed impossible to the girl getting off the plane from New York which had just taxied into the Atlanta airport that such a thing as New York and a real southern plantation could actually co-exist in the 1950's.

In the late summer she had met Ruthanne Reeves on a vacation trip to Greece and the two girls had returned to New York on the same plane. Ruthanne went back to her plantation home in Georgia and Elise Barnhardt to her work with a New York publishing firm.

Ruthanne and "brother John" as she called him, greeted Elise gaily and as they walked toward John's tiny sports car brother and sister kept interrupting each other with talk of parties and plans for the weekend. The car sped along one country road after another, seldom going through anything but villages with a few houses and a country store or two at the crossroads.

It was dusk and for a few minutes there was that

intense light in which everything takes on a glow all its own. The fragile, spider-like cleome flowers in front of the dark gray unpainted little shacks were a vibrant pink. The cotton fields could not have looked more green.

There was a dreamlike quality about the drive as they passed one shack after another with their rusty tin roofs, sitting lonely, back from the road in the midst of a few pine trees. Then they turned down a dirt road and drove through swamps which hummed and chirped with dusk's surge of life, past gates protecting private roads, and on and on. Finally, they turned down one of these, passing through an open iron gate. Sweet gum and pine branches flicked the side of the car until the woods abruptly ceased.

Ahead lay a long avenue of moss-draped live oaks and beneath these huge olds trees it was always twilight. Under this leafy, moss-draped ceiling a shadowy stillness had settled in broken only by the occasional, mournful sound of a dove.

The last rays of the sun disappeared as the car pulled up in front of an immense, sprawling southern mansion. Tall columns at the front and wings at each side made it look like some grand and dignified creature crouched nobly on its haunches. Lights were flickering on now in the rooms of the house and as the three young people entered the large center hall Ruthanne's mother, a short, cheerful little woman, plump as a marsh hen, greeted them warmly.

That evening friends arrived from nearby towns and plantations for an extremely gay dinner party and dance on the rear piazza which overlooked the river. Elise was entranced. She watched the shimmering trail of the full moon on the black waters of

45

the river with a delightful young man who managed to make her feel completely feminine and devastatingly attractive.

The party was over shortly after twelve and the girls were tired, so by one-thirty all was quiet. Elise should have fallen asleep quickly but she did not. Her trip, the events of the evening, and even the quiet, so different from all the noises of a city at night, were enough to make her more wakeful. She tossed restlessly on the high fourposter mahogany bed, heard the grandfather clock in the hall strike two and swung her feet over the side of the bed, deciding to get up and draw back the drapes slightly, hoping for a cool breeze.

At that moment she heard a clatter outside which to her startled ears sounded like the clatter of horses' hooves. Reaching the window she drew the drapes and looked out. She could hardly believe her eyes. Directly beneath her window in the circular drive stood an impressive gold and black stagecoach drawn by four gleaming black stallions. Beside it stood a coachman dressed in black coat and britches. The entire scene was illuminated by the light of the full moon. Holding the door of the coach open with one hand, the coachman gestured toward the house with the other and called out—"Room for one more!"

Amazed, she stared down at his face. The skin was swarthy and the lips full above the jutting chin. A long scar staggered irregularly across the man's left cheek, running from the corner of his eye to his mouth.

Before she could recover from her surprise both coach and coachman seemed to literally dissolve into the darkness and disappear. She did not fall asleep until the day broke, she was so frightened, and the next morning she was quite late in awakening.

Ruthanne teased her about the young man she had danced with so frequently the night before and whether she had not tired herself out. Elise smiled somewhat wanly. She was embarrassed yet she felt that she would be more so, if she tried to tell her friend she had seen an old-fashioned carriage and coachman in front of the house in the middle of the night.

That evening everyone gathered again to swim in the river and cook supper along the shore. They were all warm and friendly but as it grew dark, Elise found herself growing somewhat depressed and uneasy; however, she forced herself to talk and joke and somehow the evening passed. At eleven everyone left and the two girls sat down over a glass of iced tea and cookies to talk. But soon Elise felt so irresistibly sleepy that she could not stay up any longer so she told her friend good night.

She fell asleep almost immediately and when she awoke, although it was only about an hour later, she did not know where she was or why she had waked up. In a moment or two she recognized the tall bedposts in the light from the moon streaming in the window and realized she was not in her New York apartment but in the bedroom of the plantation house. From without there came the rhythmic clatter of horses' hooves. She got up quickly and went over to look out. There below the window was the same scene of the night before, the striking black and gold coach and the figure of the coachman standing beside it, holding the door open with a flourish.

"Room for one more!" she heard him call out and tonight as he did so he looked up toward her window and smiled. But the smile was horrifying and made the scar on his cheek stand out with an almost purplish hue in the moonlight. "Room for one more," came the call again and this time the invitation seemed to be meant for her!

Then the coach vanished as mysteriously as it had the night before. Elise was so terrified she literally began to tremble as she sat on the edge of her bed. She did not know whether to leave her room and awaken Ruthanne or whether she would be able to conquer her fear and wait until morning. She went back to the window and looked out but where the coach had stood there was now nothing at all except a pattern of shadows cast by the moonlight upon the white gravel of the drive. A breeze rustled softly through the magnolia leaves and other than that, most of the small night sounds seemed to have fallen asleep. All was quiet and finally Elise, too slept.

The following morning Elise was so exhausted that it was not hard for her to convince Ruthanne she was not feeling well and would like to return to New York. Ruthanne and John were disappointed but considerate enough to help her in every way. Elise had not been able to get a reservation from New York on the flight she wanted. Now she insisted she would go on standby.

When they arrived at the airport she bought her ticket and was told that even though the plane was full, there was always the chance a passenger might not arrive. No one else had gotten there before her to stand by and she would have the first available seat. They watched the big silver plane taxi up. Passengers got off and other passengers with their reservations got on.

As she walked toward the gate she saw the retreating back of the attendant going to the plane to check with the stewardess on whether it was full. She chatted with John and Ruthanne more cheerfully now that she knew she was away from the plantation and would be back in her own apartment that night. This busy airport seemed far away from the world of the Old South as she waited to see whether she would get a seat. Now the gate attendant was returning from checking to see whether there were any empty seats. She heard him call out.

"There is room for one more."

Elise felt a sense of shock go through her entire being. She moved forward so that she could get a better look at the man's face and as she did so he looked directly at her and repeated, "Room for one more!" His eyes met hers and there was a strange half-smile in them. His skin was swarthy, the lips full and red above a jutting chin. A scar ran across his left cheek. It was the face of the driver of the coach! The coachman who had come for her two nights in succession.

Almost hysterical, she asked her friends to take her back to the waiting room. She knew that she was not going to take that plane no matter how eager she was to get home. There was nothing she could do now but tell Ruthanne and John about her experience of the past two nights and they were astounded for neither of them had ever seen the coach or the mysterious coachman, and the plantation had been their home since childhood. However, they were quite sympathetic and it was decided that Elise should wait for a later plane and meanwhile the three would have dinner.

When it was time for her plane to depart they went back to the same gate. All three were curious to see whether the same attendant would be there. Instead they saw a thin, blonde young man with a lightly tanned complexion and a pleasant smile looking over the group of people huddled near the gate waiting for the plane to fill and hoping for a seat.

"Where is the other fellow who has the scar across his face?" Elise asked the gate attendant.

"What fellow with a scar on his face?

"He was here for a flight to New York which left from this gate at twelve-thirty," Elise replied.

"That's impossible, I remember being on this gate myself because when I went to the plane to check on the number of passengers, I was delayed getting back. I stopped to help the stewardess with a door which was sticking. When I did return and called out that there was room for one more, a man with a briefcase under his arm got on the plane. We don't even have anyone like you describe working for us, miss."

Elise told her baffled friends good-by and got on her plane. The take-off was a beautiful one and the trip back to New York uneventful. that night she was too exhausted even to wonder about the strange events of the weekend. She decided she would think about them later and went on to sleep. The next morning she opened the door of her apartment to bring in her milk and morning newspaper. Glancing at the paper she saw the headline "Plane Crashes on Way to New York."

She read the story. The plane had left the same airport she had early yesterday afternoon. It was the flight which had "Room for one more!"

Tavern of Terror

It was a stop on the drover's trail along the winding French Broad River . . . but for some it was the last

There is a stretch of river on the French Broad from Painted Rock near Hot Springs to a place near Marshall, North Carolina that is one of the most beautiful, scenic and wild valleys of eastern America.

It is also a haunted land, eerie even while the sun casts shadows upon the high cliffs and reflects dancing lights upon the river's waters. Standing down by the river's edge one can hear the echoes from the past, for it was here that the drover's trail ran south from Tennessee following the winding course of the French Broad. Herds of cattle, flocks of geese and turkeys passed through this gorge on their way to market in South Carolina.

And every half dozen miles or so along this stretch of river, there was once a tavern or inn where the weary traveler could rest. Almost all of these tavern people were honest men, good hosts, caring for men and cattle alike. But there was one tavern along the

Clarkson laid his gold watch and chain on the bench beside the lantern

river that was not like the rest.

And should you walk today along the banks of the river near the site of this tavern you may still hear the cries of the ghosts of murdered men.

But now let us tell you why this stretch of river will forever be haunted by its past.

The white sarvis trees were in bloom and it was a beautiful day that Spring afternoon of 1864 when Clifford Young rode into the little town of Marshall, North Carolina. Surrounded by steep purple mountains, the homes perched precariously on stilts against the side of the cliff.

The traveler had made up his mind that since there were at least two more hours of daylight, he would seek lodging on the drover's road and stopped to question the first villager he met about a place to stay overnight.

"Wall, I reckon you might say Chunn's Tavern is nearest," the mountaineer replied. "That is if you ain't afeard to stay there."

"Afraid? Why should I be?" asked Young curiously.

"Oh, no reason 'cept them that stays there ain't always heered from again—least not in this world. Some folks says the place is haunted."

Young could hardly refrain from smiling at this bit of mountain credulity, and after asking the distance to the "haunted" hostelry he rode on through town. A few minutes later his horse was trotting cautiously along a steep and rugged path. Ordinarily darkness held little fear for this ex-soldier who had lived through the horrors of the Confederate retreat from Nashville. But as night began to close in around him in this densely wooded hill country, he could not shake off a feeling of apprehension.

His eyes strained to see ahead in the fast deepening

twilight. Heavy undergrowth fringed the trail at either edge and horse and rider seemed to share a sense of dread as they passed through the gloomy depths of the woods.

A shrill cry shattered the stillness. Young started, then reined his mare in more tightly just as she stumbled and almost lost her balance. For a moment the animal stood still, gave a nervous whinny and then continued to climb.

He could only conjecture that the cry had been that of some animal, perhaps a wildcat. But try as he would to suppress such thoughts, Young's mind kept returning the the mountaineer's warning. He could not dispel his depression.

It was in this mood that the finally rounded a bend in the trail and saw Chunn's Tavern for the first time. There it stood, a huge monstrosity of a building, crouched with its back against the mountainside. Across its face ran a long, overhanging porch. Dim strips of light showed through the shuttered windows. And beside the front door hung a perforated metal lantern like a malevolent eye emitting sparks of hate.

Young's first thought was that the tavern's appearance lent itself well to the mountaineer's tale. But he upbraided himself for such foolishness and, dismounting, lifted the large knocker on the door. It was opened almost immediately by a short, heavyset fellow. And with a hearty familiarity which Young found most repellent, the man ushered him in.

"My name is Chunn and we are so delighted, so delighted to have such a gentleman as yourself stop with us," greeted his host unctuously. Chunn's manner and vacuous looking face filled Young with revulsion, but at least his fears were groundless. Certainly, a man of this sort was far too servile to be dangerous. Such a manner was more often found in cowards.

Chunn introduced him to his wife, a scrawny woman with piercing black eyes who preceded him up the stairs and to his room. As it was seven o'clock, Young decided that he would sup in the main room below and come back up to bed immediately thereafter. Tomorrow's ride would be a long one.

The huge fireplace with its blazing logs radiated warmth and made the dining room of the tavern unexpectedly cheerful. Young forgot his somber thoughts of a short while before and gazed curiously around him at the other lodgers.

His eyes fell first on an overdressed, bumptious pair whom he guessed might be a sutler and his wife. Her bonnet was laden with feathers and furbelows and from beneath its brim stared tiny, gimlet eyes made smaller by the puffy folds of flesh around them. Her trader husband was as grossly corpulent as she. And his face looked as if a huge hand had been stroked downward upon it blurring any traces of character it might once have had.

At another table sat a rough looking fellow who still wore the cape style army overcoat of the Union forces. But Young had a suspicion it had been borrowed without leave from some unlucky Yankee. The man was determined to avoid his eye.

The most sensitive and intelligent face belonged to a young man with a russet beard who sat nearest him. His clothes gave off an air of quiet elegance, a bit startling in this isolated mountain area. At this moment the young man arose and walked over to his table.

"I would guess from your bearing, sir, that you

have been a military man. Is that true?"

Replying courteously in the affirmative, Young invited him to join him. His name was Clarkson, and he proved to be a Virginian like himself. One might judge from his dress that he was extremely well-to-do. Young was particularly struck by the heavy gold chain and handsome watch which Clarkson wore.

The two men must have talked for over an hour when they noticed it was getting late and, both wanting to make an early start the following morning, they bid each other the friendliest of good-nights and retired to their own quarters.

As Clifford Young unlocked the door of his room he heard a footstep just behind him. Wheeling around he saw the rough looking fellow he had noticed in the dining room. Still in his army overcoat he scurried past and ducked furtively through a door a short distance down the hall. What was behind the man's strange manner and why had he attempted to avoid his gaze in the dining room?

57

Young puzzled over it as he lay in his bed leafing through the pages of his Jefferson's Bible. He must have read later than he realized for when he turned down his lamp, it was half after eleven. He had just begun to doze off, comfortable under the warmth of the heavy quilts, when he heard it. His whole body tingled with horror. He heard the sound of a man's screams, screams so fearful that all the dark corners of the mind must have joined hands and forced their way out through a human throat. There was a dull thudding noise and then—silence.

Clifford Young jumped from his bed and as he did so his own lamp flickered out and he found himself in total darkness. For a few seconds he stood tensed, half expecting some intruder to throw himself upon him from the blackness. But nothing happened and finally his fumbling fingers grasped the doorknob. He flung it wide open and there, squarely in front of him, stood Mrs. Chunn, her eyes wide and enigmatic.

"Oh, you are awake, sir. How you did startle me throwing the door open that way."

"Madam, where did that screaming come from?"

"Screaming? I didn't hear anything. Perhaps one of the gentlemen had a nightmare."

As young started to move past her into the hall, the woman stepped almost imperceptibly to one side so that he found his way blocked. For a moment they stood staring at one another. Then, loath to argue with her, Young turned and went back into his room. But there was no sleep left for him that night.

He arose very early and, dressing quickly, ate breakfast and left Chunn's Tavern. Mist still hung over the mountainside making it hard to see any distance ahead. The sharp turn in the trail was upon him before he realized it as he rode along. He heard a crackling sound in the brush but took it to be a fox or a rabbit. Then and utterly without warning came the sharp report of a gun from his right. Recalling a trick he had used to advantage during the war, Young allowed himself to fall from his horse as though hit and his hand came to rest on his revolver.

The figure of a man emerged from a thicket and as it did so Young drew aim and fired. His assailant fell. Leaping to his feet with his revolver still pointed at the figure on the ground he advanced cautiously. To his amazement, he found what appeared to be the body of a dead Negro man. As he turned him over Young saw something glitter in the half light of the early morning. And out of the dead man's pocket fell a gold watch and chain. It was the watch and chain Clarkson had worn the night before.

Anger swept over him like a torrent and his first thought was to get back to the tavern. He rode with the abandon of a madman and wrenching open the door called out to Mrs. Chunn.

"I have just killed the man who murdered Clarkson. What do you know of all this?"

The woman stood stone still, her face ashen.

"My God!" she screamed. "You have killed my husband!" And with that she ran out of the tavern and up the trail.

For the first time the realization of what had actually happened took shape in Clifford Young's mind. He knew now the fate of the guests at the "tavern of terror." His friend, Clarkson, had died at the hands of the Chunns the night before, and prosperous looking guests who were not done away with at the tavern were waylaid on the trail. Where the trail turned made an ideal place to ambush travelers and Chunn, himself, had lain in wait for him that morning, blackening his face as a disguise and attempting

59

to murder him. This time Alfred Chunn had met his match.

His and his wife's game of death with their hapless lodgers was over forever. But for many years afterwards riders along this isolated mountain road often reported hearing wild cries and seeing eerie figures appear suddenly in front of them. It is not surprising, for if the spirits of those who die a violent death are restless and prone to return, there are many with a reason to haunt this road. And, certainly, the evil spirit most likely to wait and watch and linger on out of the past is the ghost of Alfred Chunn himself.

If you should go this way at night, look for him. He may be looking for you.

The Surrency Ghost

A railroad ran special trains for people to watch these strange happenings of the supernatural

It is doubtful whether one person in a thousand driving down Highway 82 through Jessup, Georgia, knows that they are close to the site of one of the strangest supernatural occurrences on record.

Terrifying events took place at the plantation of Millard Surrency despite his reluctance at first to discuss them. From 1872 to 1877, thousands of people visited "Surrency," including scientists bent on explaining away the events and reporters sent from their newspapers to investigate. A railroad even ran special trains for people to watch such predictably regular exhibitions of the supernatural.

One summer afternoon in June of 1872, Mrs. Surrency sat quietly sewing in her bedroom. The beautiful mahogany headboard of the four poster bed gleamed in the light of the sunshine which streamed through the window. Her husband, Millard, was pleased with the stand of cotton on the plantation.

The children were enjoying the swimming, dancing and exchange of visits, all part of the pleasures of summer. Mrs. Surrency could not have been happier.

As she sewed a feeling of contentment pervaded her and she didn't notice a noise behind her. It came again and she looked around the room but saw nothing. The third time she realized that it came from the washstand behind her which was near the head of the bed. She stopped her work and gazed at it curiously. To her amazement, the pitcher in the washstand bowl at first almost imperceptibly, then with greater agitation, began to rock back and forth. Gradually enough momentum was generated so that it actually inscribed an arc over the side of the bowl and landed upright beside it on the washstand. Mrs. Surrency was now sure that one of her boys must have tied a string to the pitcher and be playing a trick upon her. She examined the pitcher, but there was no sign of any string.

Ann Surrency was calm of temperament and her first reaction was more that of puzzlement than fear. She had just turned toward the door, wondering where the boys were, when a loud crash came from behind her. Turning she saw the floor in front of the washstand covered with fragments of china and glass. The bowl lay in a thousand fragments at her feet. Pieces of the matching china soap dish were there, too. Even the hand-painted glasses at the back of the stand were now nothing but sharp, silvery slivers along the debris scattered upon the dark floor.

While Mrs. Surrency stood in astonishment gazing at the remains of her once lovely toilet set, she happened to look over at the washstand just as the pitcher began to rise slowly into the air. As if tilted by some invisible hand, it remained poised while the

water it contained was poured slowly out upon the rug. Then with a kind of savage flourish it was lifted high and flung to the floor.

Mrs. Surrency ran from the room.

The first person she met was her sixteen-year old daughter, Clementine, and son, Millard, Jr., who had come into the large center hall. They were calling her to settle an argument as to who was to ride their father's handsome new stallion, Sea Horse, first. Both hushed quickly when they saw the expression on their mother's face.

She told them what had happened and during the conversation their father came in from his morning tour of the plantation. After some discussion everyone tended to think that the entire incident was probably the result of an earthquake tremor. So they dismissed it from their minds.

The next day as the family were together for their mid-day meal, a door which opened on the long gallery at the side of the house closed with a loud bang. The entire family jumped at the unexpected noise, then agreed that it must have been the wind.

"Perhaps we are going to have a summer storm," said Mr. Surrency, folding his napkin. As he did so the Surrencys heard the same heavy door creak open and close with such a violent crash that it almost shook the house. Young Millard pointed speechless at two of the dining room windows. The two windows which had been raised were now edging downward simultaneously. They struck the sills and began to go back up faster until as they opened and closed loudly several times some of the small panes were shattered.

Clementine began to cry. Her mother tried to sooth her. Young Millard went over to check the windows while Millard Surrency, Sr., and his older brother Robert ran out of the dining room toward the gallery. They could see no one, and a thorough search of the grounds near the home revealed nothing.

Entering the separate kitchen back of the house, Mr. Surrency found the family butler and cook. Both looked extremely frightened. Maggie literally shook, and the pair seemed as puzzled by the racket as the Surrencys.

This was only the beginning. From then on many strange and frightening incidents took place, although they seemed to be restricted to Mrs. Surrency's bedroom or the dining room. On several occasions the family sat down to a beautifully set table and appetizing meal and before there was sufficient time for the family to bow their head for the blessing, the table cloth with the serving dishes, plates, crystal and everything upon it would be snatched from the table. The food was unceremoniously dumped into the Surrency's laps and on the floor.

Even when the Surrency's meals stayed on the table there was a continual succession of other minor, although sometimes painful, disasters. Hot tea, coffee, or soup was often flung in the faces of various members of the family. Their forks or spoons sometimes broke in two or were twisted out of shape even as they held them in their hands.

It was not long before the events, first confined to Mrs. Surrency's bedroom and the dining room, began to spread throughout the house. Doors and windows would slam, furniture would begin to move in an eerie dance about the room, then back to its place, or fall forward with a crash which sometimes shattered valuable family pieces. There was an ever-present danger for the children as heavy wardrobes and bureaus tended to suddenly topple forward, and mirrors and pictures frequently fell from the walls.

These weird phenomena went on during the night as well as the day until the entire family barely ate or slept, awaiting the next shocking event.

For some reason the manifestations seemed to single out young Clementine for the most lurid and dramatic demonstrations. If she touched a table, when she withdrew her hand the table followed her, floating along perhaps a foot above the floor. If she sat in a chair, when she arose the chair would trail her throughout the house. It was a strange sight indeed to watch Clementine Surrency go down the stairs, through the house and out to the garden with a chair floating right along just a few feet behind her.

Even worse, it became so that Clementine could scarcely enter the room without all the furniture lifting from the floor and engaging in a weird, maniacal kind of dance, whirling here and there for as long as five minutes at a time, until suddenly all became still. Or one would crash with incredible ferocity into another, wrecking some beautiful family heirloom.

The Surrencys discussed moving to another plantation which Mr. Surrency owned, but they had spent many happy years in this house built in the 1840's and they were reluctant to leave.

Mrs. Surrency became increasingly alarmed over the physical safety of the children and that of Clementine in particular. Invisible hands would tug her hair roughly, her bedclothes were snatched from the bed. Sometimes as the girl was about to go to sleep, her bed would begin to rock violently to and fro as if attempting to throw her out of it. Early one morning in February, she was lifted entirely out of bed just before the incredibly heavy canopied bed was overturned, falling sideways on the floor with a horrendous crash which awakened the entire household.

That day the family made up their minds that they would move to the other plantation as soon as they could pack their belongings, a matter of a few days. But the move was not destined to be made in so leisurely a fashion. For that very afternoon the danger of the malevolent force at work in the Surrency house showed itself most clearly. As young Sam Surrency walked into the library where his brother Robert sat quietly reading in a chair before the fire, he saw one of the huge brass andirons lift itself from the flames into the air. For a moment it poised itself as if gathering every possible ounce of force. Then the massive andiron hurled itself through the air in the direction of Robert's head who sat unsuspecting in the chair. Before Sam could reach him the andiron had dealt Robert a glancing blow on the head. Sam tried to grasp the andiron but it was wrested from his hands and again struck Robert. This time the boy ran for his life. But the andiron followed, striking him viciously until he fell unconscious to the floor in a pool of blood. The andiron then rose into the air and, moving down the wide center hall, re-entered the library and settled itself back in the fireplace.

That evening the Surrencys, with the help of friends, moved Robert and the rest of the family to the other plantation, closing the old homeplace and taking only their clothes. The other house was furnished also and in addition there was the thought in each one's mind that the old furniture was unwelcome in new surroundings. Robert's wounds became infected and illness followed.

For almost two weeks the emotionally exhausted Surrencys recovered from the habit of jumping at every slight sound, not knowing what would soon follow. Broken limbs, wounds and bruises healed. Many of these latter were suffered by the children who had been caught beneath falling cabinets, wardrobes, et cetera.

But emotional stability had only begun to return

when all the nightmarish events descended upon them again. For a few days the family did not talk about it with outsiders, but they soon became desperate. As word of the Surrency ghost spread many distinguished people came to investigate such as Bridges Smith, Mayor of Macon, and Henry Pendleton, Editor of the Macon *Telegram*. Many reliable people, neighbors who lived near Jessup, Georgia, saw these weird phenomena take place.

Finally, the well-known medium and clairvoyant of the day, Foster, visited the Surrency home with some of his friends and remained for a week investigating. He reported that he had been in contact with spirits who told him the entire Surrency family was strongly mediumistic, especially Clementine. These were the type of people, said Foster, which spirits sought out to convey their messages to others. The Surrency family took little stock in Foster's explanation.

Shortly after their troubles began in their new home, Millard Surrency started building a small house on another piece of property he owned. When they were ready to move, he gave in to Clementine's pleadings to visit their old home so that she might pack up some of her belongings which she had left in the family's hasty move.

While Clementine packed her trunk in the house her father walked around looking at the grounds once more. Soon Clementine returned telling him her trunk was ready to be brought down. Even as she spoke there came the sound of crashing glass. The trunk hurtled through the closed window and shutters and fell on the lawn near them. The lid had burst open and the girl's clothes, in wild disarray, were spilling over the side and out on the lawn. And they were literally torn to shreds.

"We mustn't ever come here again," cried Clementine. She clung to her father sobbing hysterically.

"This house must certainly be cursed by some unspeakable evil," said Surrency. And from that day on none of the Surrency family ever returned. For over 45 years the house sat deserted until it finally burned.

The problems of the family ended after they moved into their new home which founded the small community of Surrency, Georgia. But the frightening phenomena which had plagued the family for so long were never solved and for years the people of nearby Jessup, who had actually seen the weird events taking place, continued to talk of them. Many had been eye witnesses to incidents which so completely violated human understanding they could only conjecture a force was at work which was in no way bound by natural laws. And to this day the ghost of Surrency has never been explained.

The King's Messengers

On rainy nights the eerie pair still roam, galloping along forever carrying a message never to be delivered

Major Ferguson leaned back against the white oak tree and reflected upon his situation.

His proclamation for the mountain men to surrender may have been flamboyant, but he never really expected it to create this kind of reaction. Hundreds of men were appearing as if by magic from over the mountains, traveling under the command of Campbell, Shelby, Sevier and others from that almost mythical land beyond Quaker Meadows, even beyond the edge of his map. They were coming to do battle with him. They were coming down to the lowlands to fight for their independence and there was an understanding among them that they would not go home until either they or Ferguson had been defeated.

For several days now he had been sending out his messengers in pairs, two by two, to alert Lord Cornwallis at his headquarters in Charlottesburg as to the situation. Not that his position on King's Mountain was that precarious, but he wouldn't have minded a regiment of the king's dragoons close enough to support him.

Ordinarily Major Ferguson was not the kind of man to worry, but somehow messengers were not getting through to Lord Cornwallis and in the cold chill of the October wind, he sensed the hostility of these backwoods people who refused to bow to the British flag or—what was more important—pay taxes.

The day before he had sent some of his best riders off but still there was no return message from Lord

Cornwallis. No need to waste any more of his good men on futile errands. Tonight he would send a couple of the Tory militia. He would select natives of the area, roughly dressed. They certainly would not get lost and if they ran into any mountain men, they'd be instant turncoats for as long as it took to get off down the road.

James and Douglas Duncan were farm born and bred. Unlettered but fairly shrewd fellows, their greatest loyalty was to their possessions and the protection the British flag might give their land.

Ferguson summoned the two brothers and gave them this most vital message instructing them to deliver it in person to Lord Rawdon or Lord Cornwallis at Charlottesburg. He warned them about the hazards of their mission, told them of the messengers who had not gotten through, cautioned them to talk to no one and then dispatched the nondescript pair on horseback.

For some time they rode along on this cold, rainy October night, meeting neither friend nor foe. After they had galloped for a number of miles without incident, they reached the South Fork of the Catawba River. They plunged the animals into the stream and with a great splashing and whinnying they forded the river. The men were relieved to find a tavern there at which to refresh themselves.

The tavern mistress had just lost her husband at the battle of Camden and the two sympathized with her volubly. So much so that she generously made their drinks extra hearty and as their tongues loosened, their braggadoccio remarks began to arouse the woman's suspicions that here were two Tories bent on mischief of some kind. Seeing they were almost ready to leave she slipped out of the room and up to the attic of the tavern where she stood by the

72

window waiting. Their horses were tethered just below her and she knew the direction they would ride in. She had just taken out a brace of pistols when the two drunken couriers appeared below her, mounted their horses and rode off. Taking aim she fired the first shot at the one on the right. Nothing happened. The other pistol fired a second later at the rider on the left. But neither man fell and the two riders galloped on, disappearing down the muddy road and into the night.

It was nearing four o'clock in the morning when innkeeper Amos Bissell near Salisbury heard a rough pounding at the door and, awakening, looked down to see what guests could be arriving at this hour on such a cold and rainy night. It was pitch black and, unable to see anyone, all he could hear was what appeared to be the loud voices of two men raised in anger.

"We should have taken a path toward the east hours ago. You don't know the way after all, you simpleton!"

"This is the way that varmint of a woman said to go."

"Well, drat her miserable Whig soul. Her advice is as worthless as the Continental Congress."

The two men lit a lantern and brought out a large map which they spread upon a tree stump. Now the innkeeper could see their horses. One man held the lantern while the other appeared to be studying it.

"We'd better ask the way again. Charlottesburg can't be fur from here," Bissell heard one of the men say.

He threw a long coat on over his nightshirt and unlocking the door to his room, picked his way carefully down the steep curving staircase, candle in hand. He stopped to pick up a flintlock pistol, just as a precaution, and began to walk carefully around the sleeping forms of his guests who lay stretched out on the floor around the fireplace.

Slipping back the heavy iron bolt on the Inn door he peered out. There was no one there. Drawing the coat more tightly around him, he ventured a few feet from the Inn, and then around the corner of the building growing increasingly curious, but he still saw nothing at all nor did he hear even the slightest sound. The rain had stopped but the ground was soft and soggy. Going over to the large tree stump where he had seen the two men spread out the map, Bissell scrutinized the ground around it thoroughly looking for prints of boots and horses' hooves. But not only was the yard of the Inn deserted, there was not a mark to be found. A strange chill began at the back of Amos Bissell's neck and traveled the length of his spine. He was just as frightened as he could be and he scurried quickly back into the Inn, bolted the front door and leaned his back against it. His heart was beating so rapidly he rested there a moment until he could compose himself.

Nor was this the last time the two riders were seen. Travelers on the road between Salisbury and Charlotte often saw the riders. Sometimes they were traveling away from their destination. One stagecoach driver said he had "given them directions so many times that he was beginning to resent the delays every time he met them."

Particularly wherever the road forked, the forms of the two couriers were often seen huddled together looking at their map to decide which fork to take. And anyone who chanced by was always hailed and asked the way to Charlottesburg.

"We must be there by morning," one of the men

would invariably say.

Drivers of the stagecoaches found that their horses became fidgety and nervous when approaching the riders, as if they sensed the two shadowy figures no longer belonged to the natural world.

So, as time went on and the war was finally won and the last British soldiers departed for their homeland, the king's messengers became couriers without an army. On rainy nights the eerie pair still roamed, galloping along forever with a message never to be delivered, the writer of the message long since dead and buried in the red earth of King's Mountain.

Settlements grew into towns, then cities, and the two riders became wary of the main roads, taking to the country lanes in their endless search for the way to Charlottesburg.

Some say you can still see them. A cold, rainy night in early October is the best time to look for the King's Messengers. For then they are most apt to suddenly appear galloping over the hill on some lonely dirt road between King's Mountain and Salisbury, two specters hurtling through the night on their phantom steeds, pausing sporadically to inquire the way to Charlottesburg. And, if by chance they should ask you, it doesn't really matter in which direction you point for even with the best of directions an invisible power thwarts and diverts the restless apparitions at every turn.

The Haunted Gold Mine

The Carolina Gold Rush could have made him the richest main the world until a ghost stepped in

They called him "Skinflint" MacIntosh and said if you happened to pass him sideways you couldn't see him. It was kind of a local joke in every country store between Charlotte and Concord that the only way you could see MacIntosh was from the front or back.

Not only skinny in size, he also happened to be skinny when it came to generosity, or at least that's what everyone said. But the old man was not concerned over what was said about him at the country stores or jokes about his appearance, for he owned the richest hill of gold between the Reed Mine and the United States Mint at Charlotte.

It may have looked like just another field of red clay on top but when MacIntosh got the report that the vein of gold 450 feet down was four feet wide, it brought the only kind of joy a mind like his could truly appreciate.

Of course, there was a problem. Even with the shaft dug he must persuade enough men to go down that far and dig in the damp darkness beneath the

surface of the earth and haul out his treasure. There were plenty of fellows to be had for placer mining on the surface. This needed men with more skill and more courage.

But Mr. MacIntosh was unworried. He knew how to do it. He sat on his hill and looked at the broom-straw, a warm, rusty color in the flow of the setting sun. He picked up a lump of red clay, pressing and shaping it between his fingers, and he could picture shovel after shovel full of that red clay turning to pure gold!

It seemed hard to believe that he had been picked, perhaps, he thought, by God himself, to become the richest man in North Carolina. Why, someday people would still be talking about the gold that came out of his mine long after they had forgotten mines like the Dixie Queen, the New Nugget and the Yellow Dog. What if the Reed Mine had been the first mine in this country to gain fame and start the Carolina gold rush, his mine would outproduce them all!

The next morning Mr. MacIntosh went to the store at Georgeville where he knew he would find not only some experienced miners from the Reed Mine but also newly arrived young men who had flocked into the area eager to make their fortunes. Standing there resting one hand on the counter and smiling his friendliest smile, Mr. MacIntosh announced he would pay half again whatever the other mine operators were paying.

"You'll have to," said Joe McGee sitting back with his chair tilted against the counter. "Who wants to go that far down to dig? No amount a' money is worth workin' for if a man don't come up at the end of the day to collect." There was a sizzling sound as he spat at the stove.

For a moment MacIntosh sensed that something could go wrong. There was his fortune and he was willing to pay high wages for men to dig it up for him but somehow these men were not jumping at his offer. Was his mine any different from the others? He alone knew it was the richest. The hairs rose along the back of his neck and for no longer than it takes a snake to flick its tongue, MacIntosh felt cold enough to shiver. There was even a flash of foreboding, but it didn't last long.

"Come up at the end of the day to collect. What are

The Mecklenburg Iron Works made the counter balance
weights now rusting on the hill over Little Meadow Creek—
site of the first gold strike in America. This land is now a
National Historic Landmark, one of only about a dozen in
North Carolina. The Department of Archives and History
hopes to open the property to the public after the restoration
of the old Reed Mine, the first commercial gold mine in
America.

you talkin'' about, Joe? It don't matter how deep a mine is. Whether it's two hundred or three hundred feet under the ground. You just brace the roofs of those tunnels up with good, hefty timber and you dig out the gold the same way. I've been down in that mine myself many a time and I've got the finest oak timbers and braces money can buy."

Mr. MacIntosh knew that was a lie even as he said it. But he smiled his biggest smile again and said, "All right, men, sign up over here, all of you who want to go to work for me Monday morning and start getting rich."

Joe McGee leaned back against the counter and said, "Mr. MacIntosh, if you got the safest mine like you say you have, and I got no reason to doubt you, then there's no danger workin' in your mine."

"That's right," replied MacIntosh. "Why, you're just about as safe down there as a man could be."

"All right," said Joe, I'll come to work for you."

Everyone was surprised because they knew that Joe was probably the best foreman at the Reed Mine and he knew the mining business well.

"But, Mr. MacIntosh, there's just one thing. You wouldn't mind paying my wife a thousand dollars if I did happen to get buried down there in your mine, would you?"

"Joe, I wouldn't pay your wife just one thousand dollars. I'd pay her two thousand!"

Well, that did it. Two thousand dollars was more money than most of the men had ever seen. Joe quit the Reed Mine that afternoon and told the boss he was leaving to work for MacIntosh. At least a dozen other men did the same thing because on the following Monday there was almost a full crew ready to go down into the MacIntosh Mine.

Soon large quantities of ore were being brought up and MacIntosh's excitement was so great these first few weeks that he even treated some of the men to a free drink in the local saloon.

The yield per ton of pure gold, after the Chilean mill had done its work, was incredibly high, it was said, but MacIntosh never told anyone exactly what the yield per ton was. Some of the men were finding sizeable gold nuggets. But most of the gold was found in fissure veins of quartz. This quartz was seldom glassy but rather milky white in color and often stained brown.

On his first payday Joe bought his wife a pair of fine silk stockings. She still worried about him and at first he had to reassure her almost daily. Finally, when he told her how safe the mine was, he would laugh and with his blue green eyes dancing mischievously, remind her that, "Why, if anything did happen to me you'd be rich, lassie! Old MacIntosh promised me himself that you would get two thousand dollars."

So, as the weeks passed and Joe returned safely each night to the little house where his wife, and then a baby as well, awaited him, her fears eased.

But, on the evening of the winter's first snowfall,

Joe did not come home at the accustomed time. It had been a cold, gray, drizzly afternoon with the fine rain turning into snow and Jennie's spirits were low. But she counted this due to the weather remembering that sometimes on a cold day, Joe would stop off with his friend Shaun O'Hennessy and buy a drink, so she refused to worry.

However, by nine o'clock she was quite alarmed. Wrapping the baby warmly, she left the infant with her neighbor and set out toward the saloon. She saw lights inside, laughter drifted out into the snow-flecked blackness and when she opened the door she was engulfed in the warm air, tobacco smoke and voices.

Tommy McSwain, the owner, walked over to her immediately. "What can I do for you, Jennie McGee?" But he was unable to answer any questions about Joe.

"No, mam. Last time Joe was in here was three nights ago. Seems like he and Shaun came in after work. Yes, that's the way it was."

"Anybody seen Joe McGee?" he called out to the men, a number of whom were looking curiously at Jennie by now, for it was plain to see she was upset.

There was a chorus of no's and Jennie left, deciding she would walk on beyond the saloon to Shaun O'Hennessy's. Mary opened the door and she could see Shaun dozing before the fire. He got up stiffly from his chair when he heard the door close behind her.

"What are you doing out at this time of night, my girl? Where is Joe? I waited for him this afternoon, but he said he was going to work awhile longer so I came on home. This back of mine's been hurtin' somethin' terrible."

"Jennie, what's wrong with you," said Shaun's

wife, Mary.

Tears streamed down Jennie's face but at first there was no sound. Then she flung herself into Mary's arms weeping and screaming.

"He's still down there. I know he is. He's had an accident or he'd be home by now. Get him out, Shaun, get him out! *Please!* Go down to the mine tonight."

"Mary, take her home and stay with her until I come and pick you up."

O'Hennessy pulled on his still wet boots which sat beside the fire, reached for his coat and hat which hung on a wooden peg near the door, and left.

Near the saloon he met Big Pete and they rounded up several other men to join them. The mine was only a little over a mile away but the snow made walking more treacherous and the little knot of silent miners tramped along through the blackness punctuated here and there by pinpoints of light from miners' cabins.

Three men passed, arms linked, singing a bawdy song at the top of their lungs. The one nearest Shaun jostled him roughly and if it had been any other time he would have regretted it for Shaun's Irish temper would certainly have blazed up. But his face grew just a shade more grim and he pressed on, ignoring the fellow.

It was cold and raw and the road underfoot which led up the hill to the mine was muddy. But there were stars out and it had begun to clear. The men trudged on, their heavy boots making a scrunching sound on the pieces of quartz and dark greenish gray rocks which lay along the roadbed.

Finally, they reached the place where the mine shaft lay and Shaun and one of the other men, each with their lanterns, started down the ladder and, with the light from the lanterns flickering on the sides of the shaft hewed deep into the red clay, down, down they went, past the gaping holes of old tunnels worked in bygone years and on to the vein the men were working now.

The two men walked the full length of the tunnel where they had worked that day and for the past several months. They called and then they listened. But there was no sound save the muffled echo of their own voices and the scraping of their boots on granite-like rock. After they had searched fruitlessly for about an hour they went back up to the surface where the small huddle of miners who had accompanied them waited.

The next day Jennie went to MacIntosh's office still certain that Joe was somewhere within the mine and asked him to send a search party to comb some of the lesser worked tunnels. Four of the men including Shaun accompanied her, but MacIntosh pooh-poohed the plan and said Joe would show up again "when he gets good and ready." Two weeks passed and still there was no sign of Joe so Jennie, convinced of Joe's devotion to her, was certain by now that the was dead. She visited MacIntosh again, this time to make claim for the two thousand dollars he had promised to pay if Joe were killed in the mine. MacIntosh suggested this time that perhaps Joe had not been so happy with married life, but to wait awhile longer. By now, Jennie and the baby were low on food and firewood and the other miners and their wives were taking by whatever food they could to share and Shaun O'Hennessy was chopping fire-wood for his own family and Jennie as well.

The next time Jennie went to the mine office MacIntosh sent a message out that he did not have time to see her. In tears she stopped by the

In the picture are Chilean grinding stones and an old stone chimney on the Reed property recently purchased by the state of North Carolina. This property had been designated a National Historic Landmark in the mid-sixties but not until the purchase of the land in the Spring of 1971 was it certain that the first gold mine in America would be restored and preserved.

85

O'Hennessy shack on her way home and Mary O'Hennessy made her stay on for some hot stew. Over and over she kept moaning, "He's dead, he's dead. He's down there somewhere dead. What will the baby and I do now."

That night it had barely struck twelve when there came a terrible rattling sound at the O'Hennessy door. Shaun pulled on his trousers and stumbled toward it sleepily. Without thinking he threw the door wide open and then he wished he had not, for before him stood the most frightful figure he had ever seen. The cheeks were a waxy chalk white. The eyes in their dark caverns looked like murky red marbles. Gaunt, clothes encrusted all over with dirt, one could hardly tell that it was a man.

Shaun covered his eyes in horror. A voice spoke.

"Ah, Shaun O'Hennessy. You were the best friend I had in all the world, and now you will not even look on me. Are you going to leave me down in the dark and the damp of the mine forever? And what about Jennie? Is old 'Skinflint' going to pay her the money for my life? What about your Mary? And the rest of the wives. Do you ken he will do any the better by them? Look at me, Shaun."

O'Hennessy lowered his arm slowly from before his eyes and peered at the specter of his old friend. For this weird spirit in front of him had once been Joe McGee.

"I heard you the night you came to look for me, Shaun, but you went down too deep. Stop at the second tunnel and go in. If you'll walk far enough, you'll find me. That's where I decided to stop and work for awhile the day I didn't go out with you. I was striking rich ore when the timber gave way and buried me. But none of that matters now. Has

MacIntosh given Jennie any money?"

"No, he won't give it to her, Joe."

"Won't give it to her! Well, blast him! Why not?"

"Says you ain't dead, Joe. Just went off and left her."

The ghost flew into a terrible rage and as brave a man as he was, Shaun O'Hennessy began to tremble.

"The liar! The greedy old devil! I'll haunt that mine of his forever," shouted the specter. Then he began to calm down somewhat when he saw the effect all this was having on his friend.

"Now, Shaun. You ain't scared of your old buddy Joe, are you? I want you to get Big Pete, Casey, Henry and Sam and come after me."

"Yeah, yeah. Tomorrow morning. We'll be there, Joe."

"No, not tomorrow morning. Tonight!" and with that the ghost vanished.

Still shaking, Shaun pulled on his boots and left. He knew he was not going down into that mine alone. He made four stops and each miner came with him after he told them about seeing Joe's ghost. Tonight there was moonlight and it seemed to Shaun that they reached the mine quickly, almost too quickly. The men were jumpy and uneasy but they were determined to find out if the specter had really been the ghost of Joe McGee. Single file they went down the ladder.

Casey walked along in front of the others watching for holes in the floor of the tunnel or loose overhead timbers. They had walked for perhaps two hundred feet when a voice spoke up and said, "I've been waiting for you, boys," and there stood the specter, white-faced, hollow-eyed and clothes encrusted with dirt.

"It's time you knew old MacIntosh is one of the

worst liars there ever was. This mine ain't safe and it never will be because them's cheap timbers and a lot of 'em are even rotten. I'm goin' to haunt this mine forever!"

The miners looked terrified but Shaun and Big Pete stood their ground behind Sam and Casey.

"Dig here?" asked Casey.

"Yes," replied the ghost, pointing toward the cave-in. "Why, I've walked all over this mine lately, watchin' you fellows, fearin' for you."

The frightened men dug for almost ten minutes. They were beginning to grow discouraged when there was a ring as Big Pete's shovel struck metal.

The metal turned out to be a pick and the handle of the pick was clutched fast in a man's fist. Shaun and Big Pete dropped their shovels and began to dig with their hands now. Within minutes they had uncovered the body of a man and the man was Joe McGee. No one thought to notice when the ghost disappeared because no one had really wanted to keep looking at it.

They carried Joe's body up on the elevator and home, and the next morning Shaun went to get MacIntosh. He told him Joe McGee was home and "needed to see him and he'd better come."

Mr. MacIntosh looked pretty startled, like he was going to call Shaun down, but instead he decided to go with him. Neither man did any talking on the walk from the mine office over to the McGee shack. There was a crow of miners standing around outside the little house looking sullen and silent. Three women were standing on the porch talking and MacIntosh made his way through several more who were gathered just outside the front door.

Shaun held the door open and Mr. MacIntosh walked in. At one end of the room was a long pine box and MacIntosh knew even before he walked over to it that Joe McGee lay inside the crude coffin. Jennie sat in the small rocker next to it holding the baby and crying quietly. She did not look up at MacIntosh.

A thousand dollars, that's what it was, wasn't it," said MacIntosh. Jennie didn't answer.

An angry murmur rose from the men.

"Two thousand, " broke in Big Pete. "You know what it is. We was there in the store the day you hired him. We know how often Jennie's been to you to get it."

MacIntosh started toward the door and the men gradually closed the way in front of him until he found himself looking up into the angry face of Pete Petroni whom everybody knew was not called "Big Pete" for nothing. He tried to go around him. "Big Pete" moved blocking his exit.

"All right, two thousand," he said gruffly. "She can pick it up at the mine office."

That afternoon Mary O'Hennessy went with Jennie to pick up her money and it was paid.

But the men did not go back to work that day, nor did they go back the next. Skinflint called an "important meeting" of all the miners. They all came and listened. He promised more money, he bragged about the safety of the mine and he said he had just forgotten how much Joe's wife was to get and that he was so sorry about it he had even given her fifty dollars more.

The men heard him out, their faces impassive. Then they got up and left. But the next morning there was still no sign of life at the mine and he learned that all of the men, except for a few who were packing to leave the area, had hired on at other nearby mines. Word had spread quickly that the MacIntosh mine was haunted, that it always would be, and when that kind of news gets out a mine operator is finished.

For several days MacIntosh visited some of the leaders among the men trying to convince them to go back but they wouldn't even talk with him. Finally, he gave up.

A few weeks later he walked up the hill and began to wander around aimlessly. He looked regretfully at the tall rock smelting furnace from which no smoke had come for days. He sat down at the edge of the huge grinding stones and sifted crushed quartz aimlessly through his fingers as if in a daze.

He had sat this way for perhaps an hour when a mounting fury began to overtake him. His dream of a lifetime was to be destroyed because of some superstitious miners. There was millions of dollars of gold in this hill, but he was never going to see it. He knew it. Somehow there must be a way to get it out.

And then, like an animal gone mad and with tears of frustration streaming down his face, he began to claw at the red clay with his fingers. MacIntosh was not the first man to lose his mind over gold.

A hundred years later the gold is still there. The miners have all left and no one would know that beneath the red clay of these Carolina hills the best and the worst in man struggled with each other in the search for gold.

If you should walk across these hills, you may still hear the wind whispering the names of these mines—the Dixie Queen, the Yellow Dog, the Blue Hill, The Dutch Bend and the Reed Mine, but even the wind does not mention the name of the MacIntosh Mine.

The Singing River

*Is it possible that there are lost Indian tribes
who went to live beneath the water?*

Late summer and autumn are the times when the
mysterious music of the Pascagoula River is heard
most often, and those who have listened to it remember it forever. Some say it is a soft humming sound,
others hear the strains of music so beautiful that it is
unearthly. Those who have heard it most clearly
have been out in a boat on the river itself rather than
the bank and have heard the strains of the music
begin gently around them and then swell louder and
louder. They were caught up and carried along by
the power and beauty of the strange melody which
yet contained a prevailing note of sadness.

Located on U.S. 90 between Biloxi, Mississippi and
Mobile, Alabama, the river is named for the Pascagoula Indians who lived along its banks, and for
many years a variety of legends has attempted to
explain the music.

One of the best known of these legends is the story
of the romance between Princess Anola who was
betrothed to the chieftain of the warlike Biloxi Indians and young Altama, son of the Pascagoula chief.
The tribe of the Pascagoula was known for their   91

friendly, peaceful ways and unlike some of the other Indian tribes, war never became a pastime with them. Although not as warlike as some, they did not escape that desire for vengeance which started so many Indian wars and even destroyed entire tribes.

The Pascagoulas held their feasts, their rhythmic dances, their burial ceremonies as did all the Indians but for the most part they were content to cultivate the ground with their primitive hooked wooden sticks, planting corn and beans and living in relative peace with their neighbors.

War was far from the minds of Anola and Altama when they first came upon each other in the forest near the Pascagoula village. Altama was quietly fishing in the river when he first heard something more than the normal sound of the water. It was the voice of a girl singing softly and blending with the noises of the forest and stream.

Altama searched the woods all around him but could find no one. Then he gazed up through the branches of the tree right over his head and there, perched among the highest limbs, was a lovely girl. He beckoned to her to come down and the two spent the balance of the afternoon sharing each other's thoughts and dreams. It was the first of many meetings and Altama soon convinced the girl to marry him.

So, one day she left the village of her father and was welcomed warmly by the people of Altama who immediately began to busy themselves preparing the elaborate wedding feast ordered by Altama's father. On the afternoon before the day of the feast a lone Pascagoula brave was out hunting some distance from the village when he heard the sound of voices talking in the Biloxi tongue. He concealed himself well and stood watching while hosts of Biloxi braves

in war regalia stole quietly past him traveling in the direction of the Pascagoula village. It was not hard for the hunter to guess that their objective was vengeance upon the Pascagoula for the loss of their angry chieftain's betrothed.

The hunter returned speedily to his tribe with news of the impending disaster, for those whom the Biloxi did not kill, they would surely take as slaves. Altama volunteered to go out alone to meet the Biloxi and offer himself to them in an attempt to save the village, but the other braves would not allow him to do this.

Soon the scout they had sent out to confirm the hunter's story returned. He brought news of many Biloxi warriors on the march, far outnumbering the Pascagoula braves, warriors who would soon descend with warlike screams and cries upon the villagers. A brief council was held and the people chose between death and slavery at the hands of the Biloxi or another alternative—the waters of their beloved river. They made their decision and gathering along the banks the old people and children began to walk out into the dark stream. They were followed by the braves chanting a death song and behind them walked Altama and Anola who embraced and then plunged beneath the swift flowing waters.

When the Biloxi arrived they found burning campfires and preparations for an elaborate wedding feast. But all was deathly still, nor was there any sign of man, woman or child anywhere about. It was a strange scene and there was something so eerie about it that even seasoned warriors found themselves tiptoeing about, looking in the doorways of the small cabins, staring at the smoking meat and warm vessels of food suspiciously if not fearfully. After making certain no one was there, they left, much mystified.

From that day on stories have been told of the "singing river," and of the people who chose death rather than slavery. The rippling, poignant song of the river has been heard down through the years and continues to puzzle those who seek to explain everything by the laws of science.

Interestingly enough, this is only one of a number of Indian stories of strange sounds coming from rivers and other bodies of water. The white man dreams of lost cities which continue to exist below the water and the Indian appears to have dreams buried deep in his memory of lost tribes and warriors who went to live beneath the water. Many of their stories mention songs of sadness or revelry still heard by those who are fortunate and perceptive enough.

As modern man considers building cities on the ocean floor one sometimes wonders whether in the dawn of mankind men were able to live underwater as well as on land and whether these legends dredged up from the dim recesses of men's minds are really remnants of his prehistoric past.

In any event, if you visit the Pascagoula River in the late summer or autumn you may be one of those who will hear the weird and plaintive song of the water, and then you can decide what it is and why it is there.

The Gray Lady

She walks across the barriers of time to warn the living

Few there are who have not heard the story of the Gray Man of Pawley's Island, South Carolina. He walks the sandy strand of that island to warn inhabitants of impending hurricanes.

But less known is the story of another South Carolina ghost called the Gray Lady and that is a shame. For she walks not on the sands of the shore but from out of the mist of history at the edge of men's minds. She walks as does the Gray Man to carry a warning from the dead to the living, a warning of impending danger and the possibility of assistance.

She first appeared to save the life of her brother, bringing the garments of a monk which enabled him to disguise himself and escape the St. Bartholomew's Day massacre. That was in France four hundred years ago and from time to time after that she appeared to descendants or intimates of the De Saurin family.

It is strange that such an old ghost should appear so young to those who see her. That a ghost could be both beautiful and frightening at the same time is not only possible—it is, it has been and it may be again for there is no proof that she has left South Carolina.

Nina Beaumont knew little about the De Saurin family in Camden when Raoul De Saurin, whom she had consented to marry, invited her there almost a century ago. It was Halloween and a gay party was assembled in one of the beautifully furnished rooms of "Lausanne," the name the family had given to their home. Among the paintings of her future husband's ancestors was one of a lovely girl in the garb of a nun. The face was infinitely sad and somehow Nina's gaze kept returning to it. She began to question Raoul about the nun and his reluctance to talk about her was soon apparent.

"It is such a wild and rainy night outside and so cheerful in this room that I want only to talk about happy things," said Raoul gently.

But this just aroused Nina's curiosity further and other members of the party joined in, begging him to tell the story. Finally, he consented.

"The name of the girl was Eloise De Saurin and she had been confined to a convent by her father to prevent her from marrying a young man who was not of her faith. The convent where he placed her was one of the most severe of the day and after she had spent only a year there Eloise died. Her death was followed shortly afterwards by that of her grieving mother. The father, Darce De Saurin, in a moment of guilt and despair, took his own life. His two sons whom he had banished because of their Protestant sympathies were summoned and arrived in time to hear his confession. He claimed that he had seen Eloise herself and his belief that she had come to reproach him led him to stab himself with the same dagger with which he had threatened the life of the

young man she loved."

"The story goes that later she appeared to the brothers, who recognized her instantly, and she left the garments in which my namesake, Raoul, was to escape being massacred. Jules did not escape and was murdered."

"So," said Raoul, "her appearances, according to family tradition, have happened each time before some tragic event in our family. She has always been seen by some member of the family and with the same expression of sorrow. But so far she has not deigned to visit any of us," he said, smiling and making light of the whole story.

The Court Inn at Camden, South Carolina where the Gray Lady was last seen is no longer standing

99

Nina, however, could not smile for her good spirits had fled and she felt both depressed and apprehensive. After the guests left she and Raoul stayed to talk awhile longer. Then she went up to her room. Try as she would to go to sleep, she could not, so, throwing on a robe, she decided to go down the hall and see if Raoul's sister was still awake. She took the candle holder from her bedside table and started down the dark hall which was illuminated dimly by the moonlight coming in the window at the end of the hall.

The hall was quite dark but she was able to make out the figure of a woman only a few feet ahead of her. Thinking it was Lucia, Nina called out gaily. But there was no response. They grayclad figure continued on its way down the hall just in front of her and now, she noticed that rather than walk, it appeared to glide! Who was this strange woman? Her diaphanous robes and shimmering veil lent a supernatural effect both frightening and intriguing. Nina was almost upon her when the woman turned and looked directly at her. The face was young and lovely but filled with sadness. To her amazement she recognized the features as those of the nun in the painting.

The nun gazed at her with tears streaming down her face and clasped her hands as if imploring her for help. Before she could recover herself enough to know what to do, the veiled figure began to grow dim and melted away like a cloud blown before the wind. Afterwards Nina could not remember whether her candle had blown out or how she had gotten back to her room.

She awoke to find herself still in her robe lying across the bed. And although it was a bright and beautiful day she was filled with foreboding. The

face of the nun was etched sharply and clearly upon

her consciousness and even if she was unable to understand the events of the night, she felt that it had been a warning, if not for her, for someone she loved. At breakfast she ate little and when Raoul began to talk about the hunt planned for that day she became very upset and begged him not to go. Finally, she told him why and he began to laugh, surprised that she could be so superstitious as to believe in an old legend. Between his affectionate reassurances and some teasing, he quieted her fears so that she waved and managed to smile at him as he rode off to hunt with his friends.

But as the day wore on she found herself restless and extremely uneasy. She was unable to enjoy the company of the other guests or even to read. Nothing could allay the nameless fears which her encounter with the nun had caused.

The hunters failed to return at the expected time that evening and not until dusk was fast settling in among the trees was the thud of horses' hooves heard. Nina and Lucia arrived first to meet the hunters. They both noticed that one of the horses was riderless but when the animal came up they were shocked to see that it carried a limp burden upon its back. It was the horse which belonged to Raoul and the animal carried the lifeless body of his master. Raoul had been shot and killed by a friend in a hunting accident.

The story of Nina's experience and her fiancé's tragic death was recorded in a family diary and found many years later in an old desk after the De Saurin home had been sold. Even when the huge house became the Court Inn strange stories were told about the place. One of them concerns a school teacher named Lula Tedder.

After her mother had called to tell her that her

father was critically ill, Miss Tedder left Savannah, Georgia to drive to her home in North Carolina. It was a rainy, foggy day to drive and the coming of darkness made her decide to spend the night at Camden, South Carolina. She remembered the huge old Inn there where she had stayed many years before with her parents.

The Court Inn, that was the name of it. Now, where had the man at the filling station said it would be? Mill and Laurens Streets, that was the address. And there it stood, shrouded in fog and rain. The big square white building with its high steps leading up to the wide veranda was just as she remembered it.

The rain fell in torrents blown by occasional wild gusts which wrenched and tore at the trees. But from within the Inn lights glowed dimly and she could not recall when she had felt so grateful for shelter of any kind.

Lula did not wonder at the fact that the lobby was empty as she walked across the dark red carpet with its old fashioned floral design. However, her eye was caught by a movement at the far rear of the lobby and she was just in time to catch a glimpse of the graceful figure of a young Catholic nun disappearing through a door. Faintly curious she glanced down at the ledger which served as a register and saw three or four other names, but none with the title Sister before it.

A gray-haired bellboy who must have been as ancient as the Inn itself showed her to a large, comfortable room and she decided to ask him if there were any sisters staying at the Inn that night. Tired as she was she felt a vague loneliness and thought a nun might prove good company.

"No, mam. We got no nuns around here," said the old fellow shaking his head vehemently.

"Now, just let me light that fire for you. The way that wind's a blowin' and a wailin' out there 'mongst them trees, we're goin' to have hurricane weather for sure, and you'll be mighty glad to have that fire."

Lula agreed and for awhile was considerably cheered by the orange flames licking hungrily at the resin rich logs of yellow pine. But the wood burned quickly and as the flames sank lower, the shadows in the corners of the room deepened. She became conscious of an acrid, musty odor and the damp chill of the night air began to seep in around her. Although she resolutely tried to ignore it, Lula was having some very peculiar sensations. No matter how hard she tried not to watch the shadows in the corners of the room, particularly the corner near the front window, her eyes kept coming back to it. As the fire grew lower the shadows seemed to leap even more frenetically. She convinced herself that the mirror over the large oak dresser was reflecting some of the flames, distorting them and causing the strange-looking shadows. So, feeling more like herself, she folded her clothes on a chair and went to bed. Lula was almost asleep when she became aware of a soft, rustling sound coming from the corner near the front window. She started up quickly and over in the corner saw the shadowy figure of a young woman.

"Who is there? Tell me who you are," Lula cried out. The woman wore gray garments and they were the habit of a nun. Most disconcerting was the way they seemed to float in the air around her. She passed Lula's bed and as she reached the bedroom door, it swung silently open before her.

Lula remembered the nun she had seen early that evening when she had registered. Why had she appeared in her room and why had the old porter lied? She threw on her robe determined to follow and force this strange visitor to speak to her. The nun moved gracefully down the hall and Lula followed calling "Sister, wait and let me speak to you, please." But the gray-clad nun neither paused nor turned her head to acknowledge that she had heard. She reached the end of the hall and with a swirl of her garments, the nun turned suddenly around and looked Lula full in the face. She was astonishingly beautiful but the dark eyes were full of anguish. Her lips parted as if she were trying to tell Lula something and she seemed to be making a sign with her hands and gesturing toward her left.

At that moment Lula heard the sound of a door open down the hall behind her and voices. She turned at the interruption and when she looked back, the gray lady was gone. Bitterly disappointed she searched the stairwell at the end of the hall and even knocked on the doors of several nearby rooms. One door came open and she saw that at this end of the hall the rooms were not furnished or in use. The young teacher was close to panic but she managed to get back to her room where for the first time in her life Lula Tedder fainted.

When she awoke she could see the gray light of dawn at the edges of the drapes and it was the most glorious sight she had ever seen. The rain had stopped, the night had fled, the corners of the room were no longer dark—nor was there anywhere a shadowy form with misty gray robes floating around her! Lula dressed rapidly and stopped at the desk to pay her bill. The clerk ran his finger down the list of guests on the ledger.

"Jenkins, Thomas, Tedder—why, that's the name of a young man who married into the De Saurin family. This Inn used to be their home, you know."

"No, I didn't, said Lula who felt impatient but managed to smile politely. She paid for her room and the man made no further comment.

She had not driven many miles when the rain began again. Opaque sheets of water struck her windshield with such force she could barely see. Finally, she rolled down the steamy window to decide where she was and whether she was still on the right road. Ahead of her the road forked and she was about to bear right when suddenly the nun's gesture and frantic efforts to tell her something crossed her mind. Had she been pointing left? Lula thought she had and without being sure why or which was the route to take, she bore left.

By mid-afternoon she had reached her home in Asheville and the small Victorian house with its green shutters was a welcome sight. As she opened the front door and walked into the hall, her mother threw her arms around her.

"Lula, I've been so worried about you. Did you know that the bridge on the old road was out?"

"No, I didn't."

"Well, it has been out since the storm yesterday and if I could have phoned you, I would have but I didn't know where you would stay. I was so afraid that you would be in a hurry and try to take the short cut at the fork."

"The short cut at the fork where the roads branch off? You know, I had almost forgotten that spot where either road brings me out at the same place. The one on the left winds about a bit more, but for some reason I took it."

"Well, they would not have brought you out at the same place today," said her mother, and she was right.

There are old residents of Camden who say the

ethereal gray lady walks on starless nights across the barriers of time to haunt the living. But always with compassion. And, if you should meet her you will know there is danger ahead. You will also know that you had a distant relative who once lived in France, a beautiful young nun named Eloise De Saurin.

The Ghost Ship

The doomed colonists saw it and so did the Indians

A lone figure stooped down at the water's edge silhouetted against the sky. It was a timeless scene that might easily have occurred a thousand or so years ago. In the late afternoon light the almost naked form of a man could be seen moving along the shoreline and gathering small shellfish. He was one of North Carolina's Hatteras Indians.

Straightening up suddenly the man gazed out to sea. Motionless and intent he watched the edge of the horizon where a small dark speck was visible. The speck grew larger and larger until the outline was the size of a toy boat, but gradually and unmistakably it became an impressive ship. Its sails stretched full and taut before the gusty autumn wind. With astonishment he saw the vessel head toward Roanoke Inlet.

He turned toward the woods cupping his hands around his mouth and then began beckoning urgently. Other Indians ran out on the beach to join him watching the big three-masted sailing ship go into the inlet. Some began to jump up and down, practically doubling up in their excitement and joy. Well

aware of how shal-
low the inlet was,
they knew the ship
was certain to
wreck. For hadn't
many wrecked like
this before? For over
a hundred years
vessels had been
going to the bottom
in inlets like this one
along the Outer
Banks and joyful
Indians had been
salvaging all sorts of
unfamiliar but excit-
ing riches including

the nails that they prized so highly.

But this time the most astounding thing happened.
With the wind behind it and the triangular flags atop
each mast fluttering, this miraculous ship sailed right
through the treacherous, shallow water with never a
pause. Then it turned and proceeded safely on
toward Roanoke Island. The Indians shielded their
eyes against the rays of the setting sun to watch. It
was an incredible sight and the bewildered savages
waiting for the ship to run aground in the shallow
water saw it become almost transparent as the afternoon sun shone through it until it faded away, disappearing before their very eyes!

Full of awe and fear they raced toward the undergrowth at the edge of the forest near the shore. A
council meeting was held which lasted until the sun
rose again. The wise men of the tribe offered many
explanations concerning the appearance of the won-

drous ship and what it meant.

Surprisingly close to the council meeting dawn was breaking upon a group of men of a very different sort, led by a highly educated, keenly observant Englishman. It was 1703 and John Lawson with a handful of companions was exploring the northern portion of coastal North Carolina, that area which later was called the Outer Banks. Lawson and his men traveled by boat along the rivers and late one fall afternoon two Indians in a canoe paddled out to their boat. One threw beads in Lawson's boat as a sign of love and friendship. Since the explorers were tired he consented to the Indians pleas to go ashore with them.

As soon as they landed they were joined by other Indians of the same tribe bringing a large store of fresh fish, mullet, shad and many other sorts, which they shared with the hungry travelers. Lawson and his men were much impressed by the friendliness and generosity of these tall, well-built Indians with their surprising gray eyes. No other Indians they had met possessed eyes of this color. Normally, their eyes were dark brown, sometimes verging on black.

After the bountiful meal was eaten under the large laurel and bay trees, it was plain the Indians were eager to tell the Englishmen something they considered of the utmost importance. The chief man among them, he who had thrown the beads into their boat, stepped forward and began speaking to Lawson. He gestured often toward the sea and spoke in such an excited manner that his story would have been difficult to follow if Lawson had not learned the language of a number of Indian tribes while roaming the

Early morning light reveals remains of wooden schooner buried in the sand near Nags Head

coastal Carolinas.

As he waved a bronzed arm in the direction of the ocean the other tribesmen stood silently by occasionally nodding vehement assent. Lawson's comrades could catch the word for "by ship," "under full sail" and "talk in a book" which was the Indian way of describing a man who could read.

Lawson's eyes shone with excitement and his men

could scarcely wait for the Indian to finish so that they might learn what he said. None of the Indians added to his story, it being their custom to listen respectfully to a speaker and not interrupt one another. When he had completed the story to his satisfaction, the Indian fell silent and looked at Lawson with unusual warmth and expectancy.

John Lawson responded with the word for brother

at the same time gesturing in a friendly fashion to assure the Indian of his feeling of kinship.

Now it was the Englishmen's turn to hear the story.

"This is not the first time I have heard of this man's experience," said Lawson. "It has been told me by many an Indian wise man when I have been in these parts of Carolina. This man says that many times their tribesmen have seen a ship they were certain was an English sailing vessel come over the horizon and sail quite close to land. It has happened during the day as well as on moonlit nights. Someone among them would look out to sea and there would be an imposing ship under full sail. Quite often it would sail along for a considerable time so that others would gather and watch the ship in amazement as it glided through the water.

"But each time they attempted to paddle out to it in their canoes, it would disappear, filling them with fear and awe. He believes this ship is the one which brought the first colonists to this Island and the Indians call it Sir Walter Raleigh's ship." Lawson stopped to admonish some of the men who were smiling.

"The truth of this has been affirmed to me by men of the best credit in the country." These men say that "several of their ancestors were white people and could talk in a book (read as white men did), the truth of which is confirmed by gray eyes being found frequently amongst these Indians and no others."

Lawson went on to recall to his men the story of the ill-fated colony which John White left in the summer of 1587 in order to bring back badly needed supplies from England. Unfortunately, upon his arrival in England in November, he found his country at war with Spain. Every ship was being commandeered for the struggle and although he begged to be allowed to return to the colony with the supplies they desperately needed, he was refused permission.

Meanwhile the colonists suffered and waited watching day and night for the ship's return. In the spring, White optimistically fitted out a small fleet to leave for Roanoke Island. But the Queen of England seized the ships before they could sail. Winning the war with Spain came first.

Those of the colonists who had been able to survive the winter were probably still hopeful. One can imagine them watching the horizon anxiously day after day expecting the arrival of the vessel which would bring the long-awaited clothes, food, medicine and ammunition to relieve their suffering. What rejoicing there would be. As they huddled cold and half-starved along the windswept shores of the island, perhaps they began to have hallucinations. Is it possible their eyes began to supply the ship they wanted so badly to see sailing along that vast, empty, gray-blue horizon of the 1500's?

Some died from sickness, others hunger and, no doubt, they felt more and more abandoned and alone. Their Indian companions who had helped them survive the winter, probably began to watch with them scanning the horizon for the ship the white men talked of constantly, lived for and were so certain would come.

Tragically enough, and despite all his determination, for after all, he had left his daughter and grandaughter on the island, it was not until August of 1590 that John White was able to return. He set sail on the *Hopewell*, one of three ships sent to raid Spanish vessels off the coast of Cuba and capture whatever cargo or treasure they could. Then they were to sail northward up the coast and aid the colonists.

At daybreak on August 18, 1590 White and several sailors got into a small boat and paddled through rough seas to shore. They walked through the woods and rounded North West Point to the place he had left the colonists three years before. White stumbled in his excitement as he climbed the dunes of sand.

At the stop of a forested dune White found a tree on which without any Maltese cross as a sign of distress, had been carved the letters 'CRO.' Bewildered, he walked down to where the settlement had been. There was the high wooden palisade around an enclosure. But the little houses inside were gone. Every building had been taken down. Scattered here and there were some iron bars and pigs of lead, some shot and four cannon. On a post at the right-hand side of the entrance he discovered the word 'CROATOAN.' White thought that this probably meant they had gone inland with Manteo and his friends to Croatoan Island and filled with excitement he wanted to go on southward to the island to look for them.

By now a storm was blowing up. The seas were so rough the men were unable even to load fresh water, the *Hopewell* nearly ran aground and the anchor rope broke so that she had lost one of her two anchors. The weather was becoming more and more treacherous so that with water and food short and only one anchor left they decided it was too dangerous to continue the search.

Completing his story about the ghost ship the Indians told of seeing and the return of White to look for the colonists, John Lawson stared thoughtfully out to sea. It was over one hundred years ago since Captain White had left the doomed colonists on Roanoke Island. Was there really such a thing as a ghost ship? And, if it did exist was it as one Indian wise man had said "an omen" to all the Indians living along the coast that they were in danger from the white man, and that the appearance of the phantom vessel was a forewarning? No one knows.

Reports which are sometimes still heard of a phantom ship sailing over the water through inlets where no real ship could ever go remain as much a mystery today as the fate of the colonists themselves.

Life boat washed up on shore of Hatteras Island

Railroad Bill

For many years this Alabama bandit eluded the law and some still see his ghost near the railroad tracks.

THE BLACK ROBINHOOD
"Railroad Bill mighty bad man,
Shoot dem lights out de brakeman's han'."

There were no screens at the windows of the little unpainted ramshackly house near the railroad tracks. But the old lady was used to that. When the sun went down the night's chill began to settle in she went to each window and hooked the wooden shutter. The old lady fastened them not only to keep out the cold night air but to keep out whatever else might be lurking in the darkness whether man, beast or spirit.

She banked the fire so she would have hot coals in the morning, although she didn't need them to start up the wood in the old wood stove for she had nothing to heat on it, no food and no money to buy food with. Since she had become too old and too crippled by arthritis to work, she had gotten a small check from the welfare but toward the last of the month there never seemed to be enough left even for food. This morning she had fried and eaten a small piece of fatback, all that was left.

She was glad to crawl under the worn quilt on the iron bed and go to sleep for that was the best way not to think about being hungry. Before long, however, she heard a shot ring out and it came from close by. A train's whistle began to emit desperate "toot, toot, toots" and then she could hear men's voices calling out and lots of shouting.

"Don't never hunt trouble," she lay there thinking and not moving. "Bad enuf to be hongry, don' have to go runnin' out to see what everythin's all about and git put in de jail, too. Dat's what happens when po' folks gits in trouble."

About that time Aunt Elly felt the house shake. It

sounded like somebody had come running and taken one big jump, landing right on her back porch. She plumb forgot the misery in her bones and was out of bed and at the back door before you could say spit. Next came a rattling and a clatter on the floor of her porch. She opened the door just in time to see a tall black man standing out there with a big grin stretched across his face, and then he was gone, a straight, broad shouldered figure running across he yard and into the pine woods.

Scattered all over her porch were cans of food and vegetables.

"God bless Railroad Bill," she said looking toward the woods and then as fast as she could she gathered every can and had them in the house and under her bed. This done Aunt Elly crawled back under the quilt. She did not have long to wait.

Soon there was a bounding on her cabin door, It shook the shack from the roof to the floor. Aunt Elly got up and opened the door. There stood the sheriff and a few men more. He asked Aunt Elly if she'd seen Railroad Bill, that he'd robbed a train and would shoot to kill. The old lady made like she was scared to death, said "Oh, mistuh sheriff, keep dat man way from heah. He mighty bad fellah an I hope he don' come neah."

The sheriff said, "Don't you worry, Aunt Elly. We'll get him this time shore. We brung along some bloodhounds. He won't bother folks no more." He turned around and stepped

The railroad telegraph sent word the freight train had been robbed

down from the porch saying, "Tell me, boys, did we bring three hounds or four? Seemed to me we took just three and now I see one more."

But no one paid it any mind and through the woods they went. The dogs were snuffin' on the ground like they had got the scent. But they came right out on the other side with no Railroad Bill in sight, and the sheriff saw the fourth hound dog had vanished in the night. The hair rose on the sheriff's neck and he turned to a friend and said, "That was no bloodhound that ran with the pack, that was Railroad Bill, instead. He's led us a merry chase tonight and he's laughin' in his bed."

For many years this Alabama bandit eluded the law. A black Robin Hood, Railroad Bill robbed freight trains along the Louisville and Nashville Railroad, distributing his loot among the poor. Some say the police finally caught him. Others say his ghost still haunts the pine woods near the tracks, and when some poor old lady finds food outside her door she is more than apt to look each way for the law and then whisper under her breath "God bless Railroad Bill!"

Near this lonely depot in Alabama, Railroad Bill's ghost has been seen walking along the tracks   **119**

The Haunted Car

They did not even want to ride in this car for something very strange had happened in it.

Most people are happy to own a new car, but recently a minister and his wife who live in Mississippi wished they did not have one. They wanted very badly to get rid of it. In fact they would even have been glad to have their old car back. It was not that this car did not run perfectly, for it did. But they did not even want to ride in it for something very strange happened when they were in this car and Bill Jamison and his wife were afraid.

It was a brand new shiny gold color four door sedan, a gift from the church Reverend Jamison had served for the past three years. After his secondhand automobile which had the temperament of a donkey about starting, along with a host of other equally endearing qualities, left him stranded half-way to a wedding he was to perform one Saturday, his congregation's natural generosity got the better of them and they decided to given Mr. Jamison a new car.

His wife, Charlene, could sit in it without the

springs jabbing her, the children could roll down the windows without the young minister having to get out and guide the glass back up with his hand if it rained, and the Jamisons began to feel for the first time that having a car was not a series of problems. All went well for the first two weeks.

It was on a Sunday night that Bill and Charlene Jamison decided they would drive to Memphis to see some friends. They were late getting off since Bill had attended a meeting at the church first and both were tired. The Jamisons were driving along from Tupelo to Memphis when suddenly a woman's voice spoke up from the back seat.

"I hope you don't mind my riding with you?" she said, and the minister and his wife turned around to find a little old lady leaning forward with an anxious expression on her face.

Deciding that she must have gotten into the car when they had stopped for gas before leaving Tupelo, Mrs. Jamison assured her they were glad to have her.

"Where can we take you?" asked Jamison.

"You are both very kind," replied the old lady. "I have been sick for several weeks and I'm trying to get to the home of my daughter who lives in Memphis."

"Why, that's no trouble for us at all," said Charlene Jamison. "That's where we happen to be going tonight. You just tell us where we can drop you off."

The little old lady seemed pathetically appreciative and gave them the street address of her daughter's home in Memphis. After that their passenger did not seem particularly inclined to talk and finding herself more tired than she realized, Charlene Jamison fell asleep.

Her husband was intent on his own thoughts and the road so he did not try to make conversation. They drove for some time in silence and it was not until he stopped at a light on the outskirts of Memphis that Charlene awoke. Feeling they had ignored the old lady, she turned around to speak to her. but, to her amazement, the back seat was empty!

Could she have fallen out of the car without their

122

knowing it? The young couple were shocked and frightened. Something dreadful must have happened to their passenger. They could not imagine how she had left the car without their knowing it. Bill Jamison turned around and drove a number of miles along the road, slowing at country crossroads where he had stopped or paused for caution lights, and the pair strained their eyes looking through the darkness expecting to see the body of the old lady lying beside the road. But they saw no sign of her.

Becoming discouraged, they decided the only thing to do was to turn back to Memphis and find the home of the old lady's daughter. They located the street and the house number she had given them and rang the bell. An attractive young housewife in her early thirties opened the door.

The Jamisons began to tell about finding her mother on the back seat of the car and their distress over her disappearance. As they told her about the old lady's asking them to bring her to this address, tears came to the young woman's eyes.

"My mother has been dead for six months," she said. "This is the third time this has happened and she has appeared to one couple several times."

It was just a few weeks later that the Jamisons decided to visit an auto dealer in Jackson, Mississippi. The salesman was puzzled.

"Now, which car is it out there you said was yours?"

"The gold colored sedan."

"And that's the one you want to trade for another car?"

"Yes," replied the minister patiently.

"Sorry, sir, I wasn't trying to be rude. But it's not often somebody brings a car in that looks like new and says they want to trade it. Been having any motor trouble?""

"No, the motor's in good condition. I just want to trade cars. There's a car over there," and he pointed to a brand new gold colored sedan.

"Yes, sir, but that's the same model you're driving."

"I know that. Do you mind telling me how much I can trade for?"

The young salesman went out and looked at the mileage on the minister's car. Then he did some figuring in his office.

"I'm sorry, but it's going to come to $750.00. You know your car does have some mileage on it and we can't sell it for new."

"I understand that. Can we finance the difference?"

The salesman figured out what the monthly payments would be and the minister and his wife signed the necessary papers.

After they were through he said, "If you don't mind, sir, I sure would like to know why you wanted to trade that car."

"Mind? No, not a bit. That car is haunted and I don't ever want to see it again!"

With that Bill and Charlene Jamison drove off in the car they had just purchased leaving the salesman staring after them, if anything more bewildered them ever. He gazed over at the car they had left behind them. Was that his imagination or had someone gotten into the car? It looked almost like the profile of a little old lady sitting on the back seat. He shook his head in disbelief and walked a little closer, but when he could see in the rear side window better, there was no one there at all.

He glanced around to be sure none of the other salesmen had seen his odd behaviour. Better sell that car before we're all crazy around here, he thought, and he walked toward a couple who had just come into the salesroom.